Practical
Sew & Mend
Essential mending know-how

Joan Gordon

First published 2016 by
Guild of Master Craftsman Publications Ltd
Castle Place, 166 High Street, Lewes,
East Sussex, BN7 1XU

ISBN 978-1-78494-176-5

A catalogue record for this book is available from the British Library.

Publisher: Jonathan Bailey
Production Manager: Jim Bulley
Senior Project Editor: Sara Harper
Designer: Ginny Zeal
Photography: Anthony Bailey

Colour origination by GMC Reprographics

Printed and bound in China

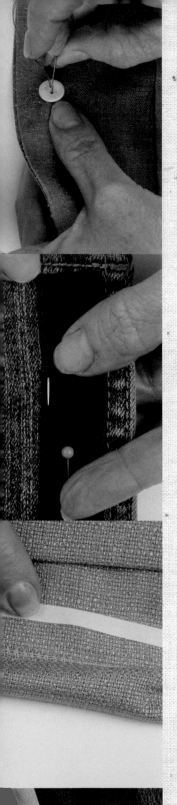

Contents

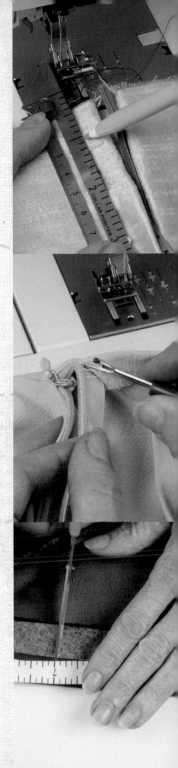

Hems

Fix and repair

Introduction

In our fast-paced modern lives, few of us have the time or the inclination to make or repair our own clothes as our parents and grandparents once did. Long gone are the days of 'make and mend', and darning old socks so that they last for years and years. Many basic sewing and mending skills have simply been lost by modern generations.

I'm sure most of us have some item of clothing that has been languishing at the bottom of the laundry basket waiting to have that tear patched up or that missing button sewn back on. And who among us, at one time or another, has not had some little clothing emergency – a broken strap or a snagged trouser hem – just when you've got a hot date or an important meeting to go to?

Well, if you don't happen to have a parent or grandmother on hand to help (or do the repair), never fear: *Practical Sew & Mend* will show you how to do it yourself. Within the pages of this book you'll find practical information on how to sew on buttons, stitch a hem, undo stitching, and so much more. When the buttons on that favourite shirt pop off or that seam splits when you're rushing to get dressed, don't ditch it; fix it and get more mileage out of your ready-to-wear wardrobe.

For the complete novice who has never threaded a needle in their life, the Basic Know-How section will guide you simply and easily through a broad range of easy-to-master techniques. For the more experienced sewer, you'll find some neat tricks for cutting corners throughout the book.

Each repair is illustrated clearly with step-by-step photographs or illustrations. Most of the repairs are sewn or fixed by hand because sewing emergencies usually happen when you're at work or play, not when you're conveniently standing next to your sewing machine (if, indeed, you own one in the first place). In other cases, such as letting down a hem, the book offers both hand and sewing-machine techniques to solve the problem.

Different sewing emergencies, such as replacing buttons and fastenings or adjusting a hem, are grouped together in separate chapters so that it is easy to find the relevant technique that will solve your repair dilemma. There's even a chapter for that ultimate emergency when you have no sewing kit to hand at all – but you'll be amazed at what you can achieve with the office stapler or a few safety pins!

This book also offers much more than just emergency repairs. If you need to adjust your clothes in any way – taking them in or letting them out due to a change in weight, for example – a range of useful techniques is provided. In addition, there are all sorts of ingenious tricks and tips for reviving your wardrobe.

If you're new to the art of 'do-it-yourself' clothing repairs, then *Practical Sew & Mend* will quickly become your sewing SOS bible.

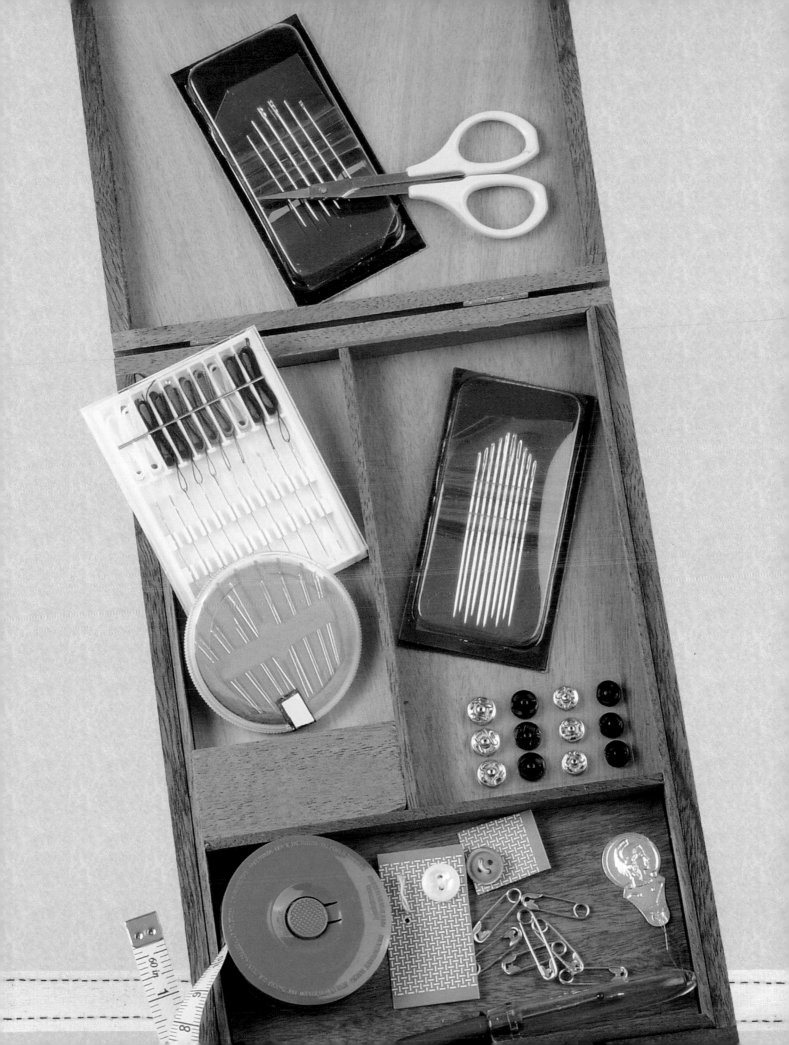

DIY Repair Kits

Stock up on a few basic pieces of equipment and sewing essentials and keep them handy in a storage box in the home for everyday sewing repairs. You may also want to make up a few mini sewing kits, to keep in the car or in your handbag, in your desk drawer at work, or to take on holiday.

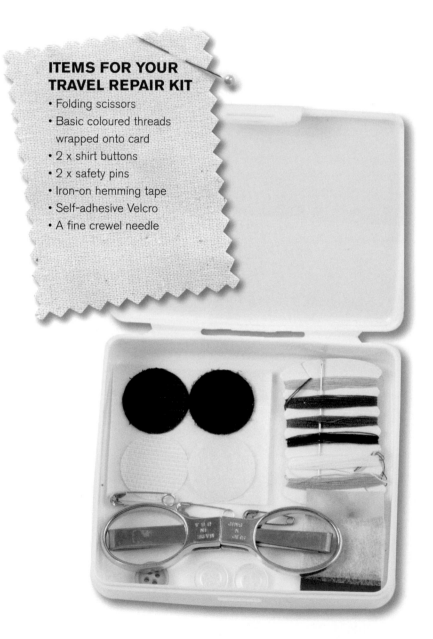

ITEMS FOR YOUR TRAVEL REPAIR KIT
- Folding scissors
- Basic coloured threads wrapped onto card
- 2 x shirt buttons
- 2 x safety pins
- Iron-on hemming tape
- Self-adhesive Velcro
- A fine crewel needle

SEWING BOXES

While department stores and haberdashery shops sell purpose-made sewing boxes and baskets these can be expensive, and there are a number of alternatives that you can find around the home. A plastic fishing-tackle box is ideal for holding lots of different small items in separate compartments. Or you could recycle an old cardboard shoe box by covering it in wallpaper or fabric to match your home furnishings. For a more elaborate sewing box (one that you would be happy to have on display) visit a craft market or your favourite junk shop or second-hand store, where you're sure to find something practical yet decorative.

TRAVEL SEWING KITS

A miniature instant repair kit can be popped into a handbag or wallet; a more comprehensive one can be kept in your suitcase or in the glove compartment of your car. These compact kits will enable most basic emergency repairs when you're out and about.

Tightened security measures at airports and other international departure points mean that even the most innocent sharp object, such as nail clippers or small sewing scissors, may be confiscated from hand luggage. Thus it is best to put your travel sewing kit safely secured inside your check-in luggage.

YOUR HOME SEWING AND REPAIR KIT

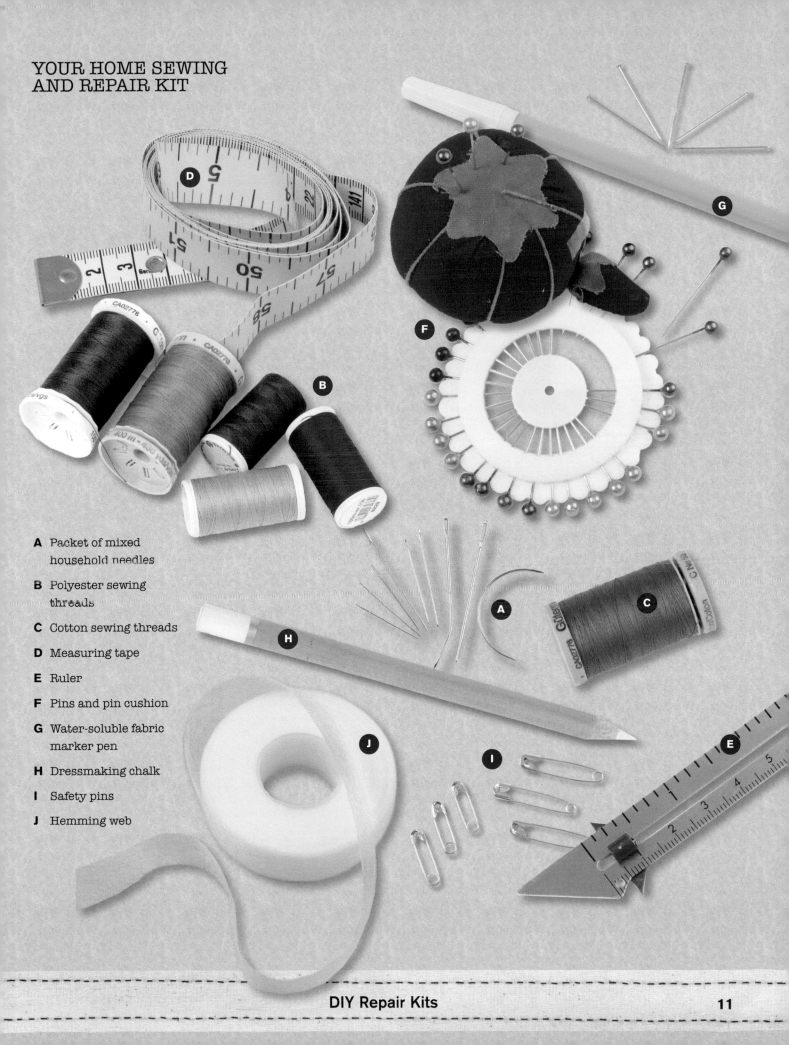

A Packet of mixed household needles

B Polyester sewing threads

C Cotton sewing threads

D Measuring tape

E Ruler

F Pins and pin cushion

G Water-soluble fabric marker pen

H Dressmaking chalk

I Safety pins

J Hemming web

Needles

The finer the fabric you are working with, the sharper and finer the needle should be. Blunt needles will snag and damage the fibres in a garment.

Polyester and cotton threads

Always use good-quality thread. Cheap threads are often made from short fibres and snap easily, causing seams to split. Reels of cheap thread usually have a slightly fluffy texture and lack sheen. Good-quality threads are spun from long strands of fibre. When you look at a spool of good-quality thread the fibres are smooth and have a satin sheen. Always test a thread before sewing with it: unwind a small section of thread from the spool, wind the free end around your middle finger and pull away from the spool. If the thread breaks immediately, it is useless and should be discarded. Polyester thread is suitable for most sewing repairs; however, if you're making repairs to linen or pure cotton garments, it is advisable to use a cotton thread.

Dressmaking chalk

This is used for marking fabric. It is available in pencils that can be sharpened. The chalk marks can be dusted or sponged off the fabric.

Water-soluble fabric marker pens

These pens can be used to mark stitching lines on fabric. When the marks are no longer required, dampen a cloth or cotton bud and rub the marks very gently until they disappear.

Hemming web

This web is a very fine ribbon of glue that melts into the fibres of material when heated with an iron. Always read the manufacturer's instructions before use.

Hooks, eyes and snap fasteners

These items are all used as fasteners. They are made from metal or plastic, come in black, silver or transparent colours and can be bought in a variety of different sizes.

Dressmaking scissors

These sharp scissors are designed to cut fabric. They will become blunt if they are used to cut paper, cardboard or plastic.

Embroidery scissors

Small, sharp and pointed scissors – ideal for snipping threads close to the fabric without damaging the stitching.

Iron-on patches

Ready-made patches with heat-sensitive glue on the back. They can be used for an instant repair, frequently to denim garments.

Decorative patches

These are embroidered patches that can be bought and hand-stitched to a garment.

Iron-on interfacing

This is a man-made fibre that is treated with heat-sensitive glue on one side. It is ironed onto the inside of a garment to give the fabric more body and stability.

Fabric glue

There are several fabric glues available on the market. Purchase one that can be used on a variety of different materials and ensure that it dries clear.

K	Dressmaking scissors
L	Embroidery scissors
M	Two- and four-hole buttons for shirts and blouses; shank button for jackets
N	Hooks and eyes: small for blouses; large for jeans, skirts and trousers
O	Snap fasteners
P	Iron-on patches
Q	Decorative patches
R	Iron-on interfacing
S	Elastic
T	Fabric glue
U	Bias binding
V	Zips: metal, invisible (nylon)
W	Self-adhesive Velcro dots and stitch-in tape
X	Thimbles
Y	Needle threader
Z	Quick-unpick/seam ripper

Fabrics

Here are some of the most frequently used fabrics in ready-to-wear fashion garments. There are so many fabrics used in the manufacture of clothing that it would be impossible to feature them all in these two pages, but the ones covered here will help you identify those used in this book.

LINEN

Linen is a durable and refined luxury fabric. It is the strongest of the vegetable fibres; it is double the strength of cotton. Not only is the linen fibre strong, it is smooth, making the finished fabric lint-free. When frequently laundered, linen becomes softer and finer in texture. Linen is made from flax; the fibre is extracted from the stalk of the plant. The lustre and sheen on linen fabric is from the natural wax content. Linen fibre can be easily dyed and the colour does not fade when washed. Linen wrinkles easily when worn but that is considered a part of its natural characteristics. Linen can be boiled without damaging the fibre (**A**).

COTTON

Cotton is a fabric that is in constant demand because it can absorb perspiration quickly, thus allowing the fabric to breath. Cotton fabric is often treated with permanent finishes to give a wash-and-wear property to garments. The cotton fibre is from the plant's seed pod. The fibre is hollow in the centre and, under a microscope, looks like a twisted ribbon. Boiling and sterilizing temperatures can be used on cotton without it disintegrating. Cotton can be ironed at relatively high temperatures, stands up to abrasion and wears well. It is often found blended with other fibres such as polyester, linen and wool to combine the best properties of each fibre (**B**).

SILK

Silk garments are prized for their versatility, wear and comfort. It is the strongest natural fibre, and because it absorbs moisture, silk cool in the summer and warm in the winter. Silk is produced by the silk worm and is harvested when in the cocoon stage of its lifecycle. The cocoons are soaked until soft, a thread is extracted and then spun. Because of its high absorbency, it is easily dyed in many deep colours. Silk fabric retains its shape, drapes well and shimmers with a lustre all its own. Contemporary silk garments range from evening wear to sports wear. Silk garments can be worn for all seasons (**C**).

WOOL

Wool fibre comes from a variety of animal coats. The fibres have crimps or curls, which create pockets that give the wool a spongy feel and create insulation. The outside surface of the fibre consists of a series of serrated scales that overlap each other much like the scales of a fish. It will not only return to its original position after being stretched or creased, but will absorb up to 30 per cent of its weight in moisture without feeling damp. Its unique properties allow shaping and tailoring. Wool is one of the most popular fabrics used for tailoring fine garments. Wool is also dirt and flame resistant. It is a resilient fibre that holds up to wear and tear (**D**).

POLYESTER

Polyester is a man-made fibre that is used in garment construction because it is strong and resistant to creasing. It melts at medium-to-high temperatures and must be ironed with care. Polyester is manufactured in many weights. Threads spun from polyester fibres are strong, wear exceptionally well, and are used extensively in home sewing and manufactured sewing (**E**).

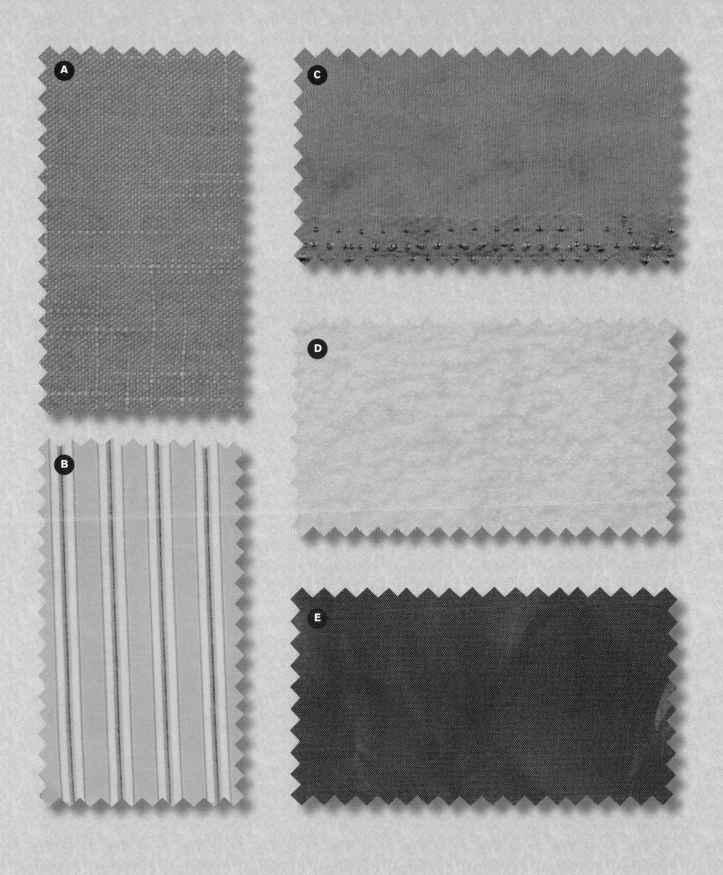

Basic Know-how

Now that you have got all your essential tools and equipment together, there are a few basic techniques and stitches that you will need to master in order to make the repairs and alterations demonstrated in this book. If you have never picked up a sewing needle in your life, don't worry: these techniques and stitches are very simple and you will be guided through step by step!

THREADING A NEEDLE BY HAND
STEP 1
Cut a length of thread approximately 18in (45.5cm) long and line the end of the thread up with the eye of the needle (**A**).

STEP 2
Slide the end of the thread through the eye of the needle and pull it through from the other side (**B**).

THREADING A NEEDLE WITH A NEEDLE THREADER
STEP 1
A needle threader can be helpful if the eye of the needle is very small. Push the wire part of the threader through the eye (**A**).

STEP 2
Pass the end of the thread through the wire eye of the threader (**B**).

STEP 3
Pull the wire eye of the threader back through the eye of the needle (**C**). Finally, remove the thread from the wire. If you run out of thread before completing your repair, knot off the thread and snip it close to the last stitch. Re-thread the needle and recommence sewing.

MAKING A KNOT (1): USING ONE STRAND OF THREAD
Often, you will need to sew with a single strand of thread. Once your needle is threaded, leave one end of thread longer than the other and tie a knot in the long end. Alternatively, sew several stitches on top of each other to secure the thread before starting to sew.

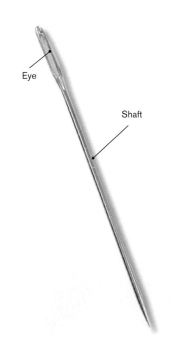

Eye

Shaft

THREADING A NEEDLE BY HAND

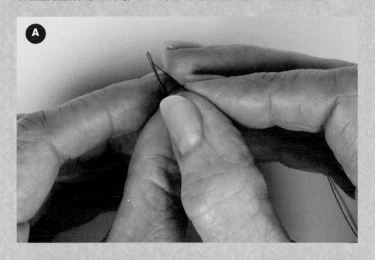

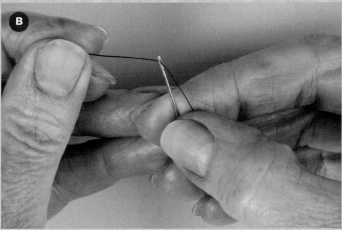

THREADING A NEEDLE WITH A NEEDLE THREADER

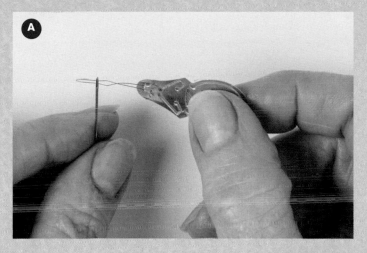

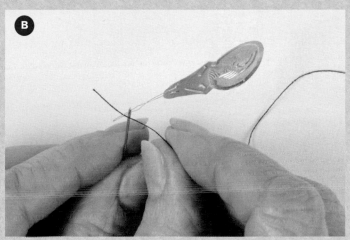

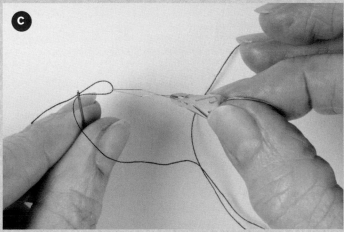

MAKING A KNOT (1)

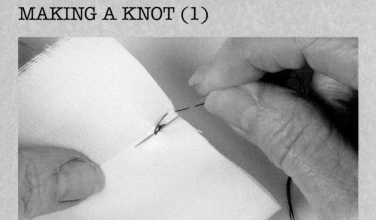

MAKING A KNOT (2): USING TWO STRANDS OF THREAD

Sometimes, perhaps when working with very thick fabric or when you are sewing through two or more pieces of fabric, you will need to work with two strands of thread for extra strength.

STEP 1

Thread a needle, as shown on page 16 and pull one thread until both ends meet. Take the ends of the thread in your dominant hand and make a small loop. Pull the length of thread to fasten the ends through and then into a knot (**A**).

STEP 2

Trim the tail of the knot (**B**).

UNDOING STITCHES

QUICK TECHNIQUE

STEP 1

Snip the stitch with the point of sharp scissors (**A**).

STEP 2

Flick the thread on the other side of the stitch up and away from the fabric with a pin or needle.

USING A SEAM RIPPER OR STITCH REMOVAL TOOL

Hold the stitch removal tool in your dominant hand. Slide the point of the blade under the stitch. Slide the stitch into the U-bend that is in the middle of the tool blade, and push the tool forwards and up slightly (**B**). The thread will be cut by the fine blade in the U-bend.

STITCHES

There are six easy stitches that you will need to learn to complete your basic sewing repertoire: straight (or running) stitch; buttonhole stitch; slip stitch; herringbone stitch; back stitch and zigzag stitch. There are also some stitches that are very easy to perform on a sewing machine.

STRAIGHT (OR RUNNING) STITCH

This stitch is used to sew two layers of fabric together.

STEP 1

Using a soluble fabric marker pen, draw the sewing line onto the fabric (**A**). This line will help you to keep your stitching straight. If you're sewing two layers of material together then pin them first to stop the fabric from slipping when stitching.

STEP 2

Bring the threaded needle up to the top surface of the fabric.

STEP 3

Make a small stitch (**B**) and then take the needle through to the other side of the fabric (**C**).

STEP 4

Leave a small space between the exit point of the first stitch and the starting point of the next stitch. As you bring the needle up to the top surface of the fabric, ensure the point of it is in the middle of the marked line (**D**). Make another little stitch (**E**) and continue sewing in this method until finished (**F**). Make a knot at the end of the stitching and trim the thread.

MAKING A KNOT (2)

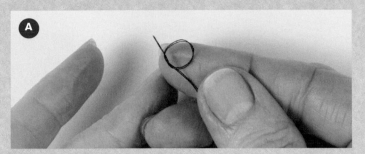

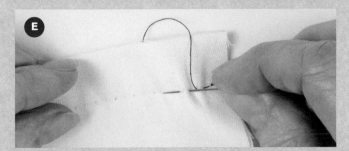

UNDOING STITCHES

STRAIGHT (OR RUNNING) STITCH

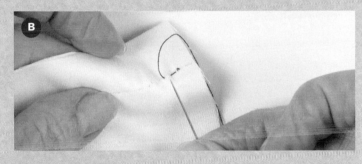

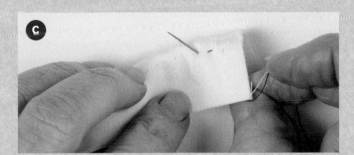

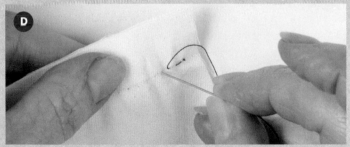

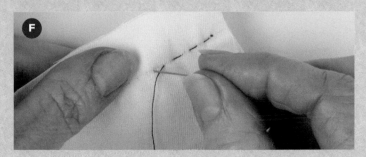

SLIP STITCH

This stitch is widely used, as it is quick and easy to sew. Use it to take up hems, sew down a gaping facing and attach shoulder pads to the inside shoulder seams of a garment.

Mending a hem with slip stitch

STEP 1

Work from right to left. Thread a needle with a long strand of thread that matches the fabric. Knot one end of the thread. Make a little stitch in the edge of the hem to secure the knot (**A** and **B**).

STEP 2

With the very tip of the needle, pick up a few threads of the inside of the garment (**C**).

STEP 3

Insert the needle under the hem edge (**D**) and pull the needle through the fabric until all the thread has been pulled through.

STEP 4

Slide the needle into the edge of the hem, making a small stitch. Move it along and bring it up and out of the hem close to the edge of the hem fabric (**E**).

STEP 5

Repeat the stitch, picking up the threads of the fabric in the same direction on each stitch. Try to sew as evenly as possible, maintaining regular spaces between each stitch (**F**). When you have finished the stitching, create a small knot on the very edge of the hem and snip off any excess thread.

BUTTONHOLE (OR BLANKET) STITCH

This stitch is used for making a buttonhole, sealing the raw edge of fabric and for attaching fastenings.

STEP 1

Thread a needle and knot one end of the thread. Working with the right side of the fabric facing up, diagonally insert the needle at the back of the buttonhole about ⅛in (3mm) from the hole's cut edge. Bring the point of needle through the fabric into the buttonhole opening. Slide the thread under the point of the needle (**A**).

STEP 2

Pull the needle through the fabric. The thread will have formed a small loop (**B**), sealing the raw edge of the fabric. Continue working stitches around the edge of the fabric or fastener. Place the stitches very close together to make a firm edge or space them for a more decorative look. When you have finished sewing, secure the thread to the wrong side of the garment with a knot.

BUTTONHOLE (OR BLANKET) STITCH

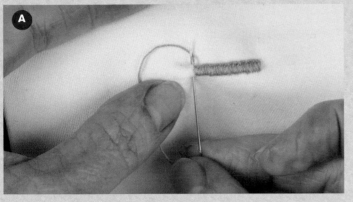

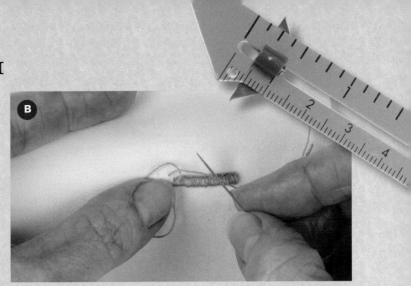

SLIP STITCH

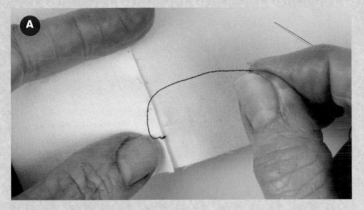

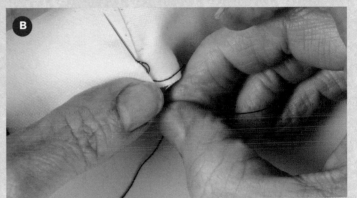

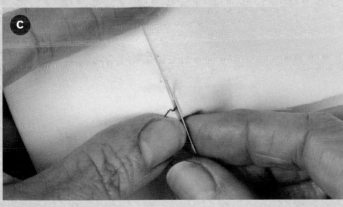

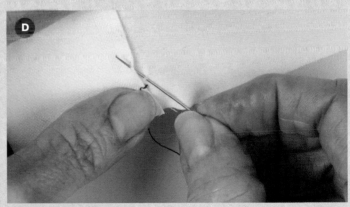

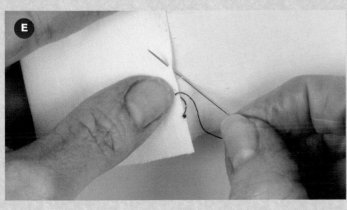

HERRINGBONE STITCH

This stitch is often used to fix a hem because it doesn't show from the front and is super strong. In addition, if you catch and rip a stitch, because of the way they are worked, the rest won't immediately unravel.

STEP 1
Work this stitch from left to right. Start sewing by securing the thread with a few small stitches to the edge of the hem.

STEP 2
Make a long, diagonal stitch from left to right across the raw edge of the hem and back through the inside fabric of the garment, about ¼in (6mm) from the hem edge (**A**).

STEP 3
With the needle pointing to the left, make a small stitch in the fabric of the hem, sewing from right to left (**B**).

STEP 4
Moving from left to right, bring the needle up and out of the fabric and make another long, diagonal stitch. As you do this, the threads should cross over each other (**C**). Continue to stitch until the hem is finished (**D**). Keep the stitches evenly spaced and approximately the same size (**E**).

BACK STITCH

Back stitch is the sturdiest and most secure of the hand stitches that are used to secure a seam or to sew two layers of fabric together. The method used for creating this stitch is similar to that used by a sewing machine.

STEP 1
Work this stitch from right to left. Sew a few small stitches to secure the thread before starting to stitch.

STEP 2
Make a small straight stitch and then leave a little extra space in front of the stitch you have just made before bringing the needle back up through the fabric (**A**).

STEP 3
Bring the needle up to the surface and stitch back towards the first stitch, filling in the space made in step 2. Take the point of the needle down into the exit hole of the previous stitch (**B**).

STEP 4
Repeat steps 2 to 3 until you have finished sewing the fabrics together (**C**). Knot off the thread and snip the excess with scissors.

HERRINGBONE STITCH

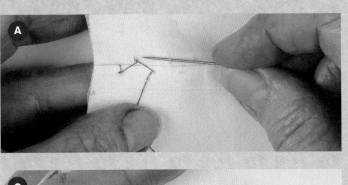

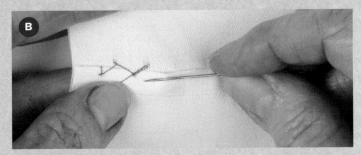

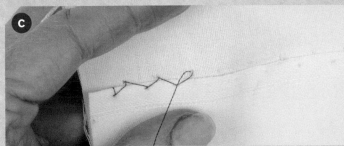

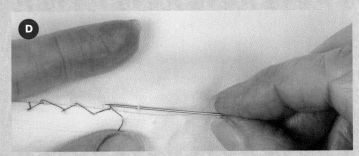

BACK STITCH

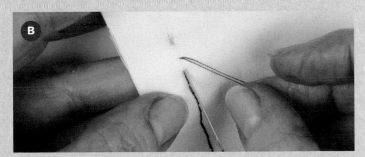

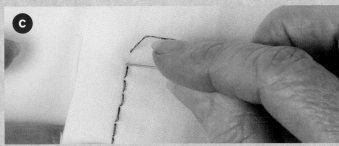

ZIGZAG (OR OVERLOCK) STITCH

This stitch is used to overcast the raw edges of seams to prevent the fabric from fraying when washed. It's also a useful stitch for joining the seams of stretch fabrics. The angle and distance between the zigzag stitches mean that seams, necklines and armholes, for example, can give and stretch without the sewing thread snapping.

STEP 1

Thread a needle with thread and knot together both ends. Pass the needle through the fabric close to the edge of the seam (**A**).

STEP 2

Make a diagonal stitch over the raw edge of the fabric. Bring the needle back up and out again through the base of the first stitch. Now pass the needle through the top of this stitch (**B**).

STEP 3

Sew neat little zigzag stitches, keeping them evenly spaced and fairly close together (**C**).

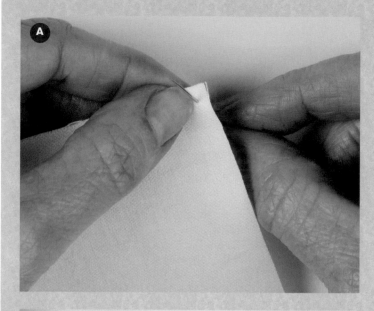

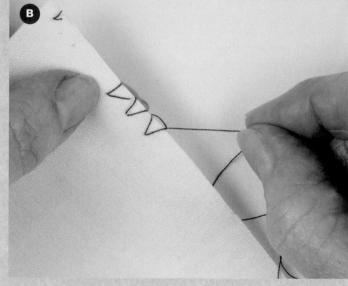

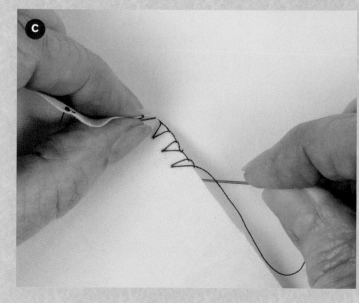

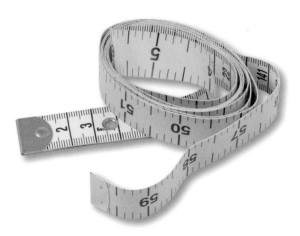

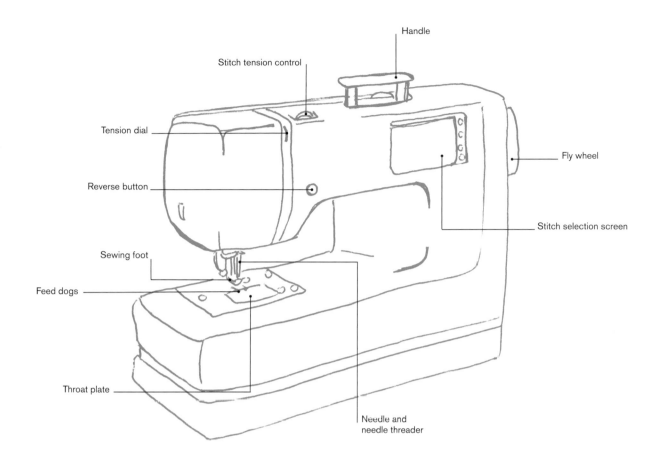

Handle

Stitch tension control

Tension dial

Reverse button

Sewing foot

Feed dogs

Throat plate

Fly wheel

Stitch selection screen

Needle and
needle threader

SEWING MACHINE BASICS

The instructions in this book assume a basic level of ability with a sewing machine so always refer to the manufacturer's manual for instructions on maintenance and particular settings. You may find the illustration above handy to identify the main features of most basic machines.

Sewing machines, like all valuable tools, need to be kept clean and regularly maintained. If you have an old machine that hasn't been used for some time, it is advisable to take it to a sewing machine technician to have it serviced. The grease that is packed into the gear case can solidify over time and if this is not checked you run the risk of the gears seizing, which inevitably ruins the functioning of the machine. It's also a good idea to check the sewing machine manual for instructions on how to oil your machine to keep it in good operational order. Various man-made fibres such as polyester

will blunt the needle, so always change the needle on the machine after every six hours of sewing. A good variety of sewing needles is vital. Purchase a case of mixed needles ranging in size from size 70, which is used for fine fabrics, up to size 90, which is more appropriate for sewing heavier weight fabrics such as denim.

If you are looking to buy a new sewing machine, then it pays to shop around. Do your homework before you buy so that you purchase a machine that will meet your sewing needs. If the machine is only to be used for repairing clothing then a second-hand model will certainly fit the bill as long as it is in good working order. Basic functions to look for include a free arm that may be removed so that you have easy access to a trouser leg or shirt sleeve and an automatic buttonhole feature. Both functions are time-saving essentials.

Buttons and Other Closures

Sewing on a Two-hole Button

Probably the most frequently experienced clothing emergency is when a button pops off a shirt. In irritation we often end up putting the garment back into the wardrobe with the intention to sew the button back on, only to never get round to it. Fix it now! You can learn how to do it here, in five easy steps.

STEP 1

Thread a needle with polyester thread similar in colour to the fabric of the garment. (The photographs show contrasting thread being used, for clarity.) Knot the two strands of thread together (see pages 16–19 for needle-threading and knotting techniques).

STEP 2

With one hand, hold the button in place where you intend it to be attached (**A**). Working from the inside of the garment, push the point of the needle through the fabric where the original button was sewn on and then up through one of the holes in the replacement button (**B**).

STEP 3

Pull the needle and thread up and out of the first hole in the button. Now place the point of the needle down into the second hole on the button (**C**) and push it through to the wrong side of the fabric. Pull the needle and thread gently until a small stitch of thread lies flat on top of the button. The needle and remaining thread are now on the inside of the garment (**D**).

STEP 4

Repeat steps 2 and 3 (**E, F**) several times, holding the button firmly in place as you stitch up, over and through the holes in the button.

STEP 5

When the button is stitched securely into place, make a stitch just through the fabric on the inside of the garment (**G**). Make a second stitch just through the inner fabric, inserting the needle through the loop (**H**) before pulling tight (**I**) to make a knot. Snip off the excess thread with scissors, close to the finished knot (**J**).

You Will Need
- A fine sewing needle
- Thread to match the fabric
- A replacement two-hole button (if the original has been lost)
- Scissors

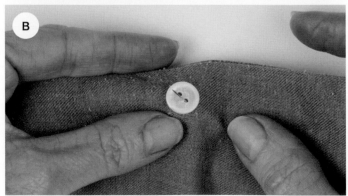

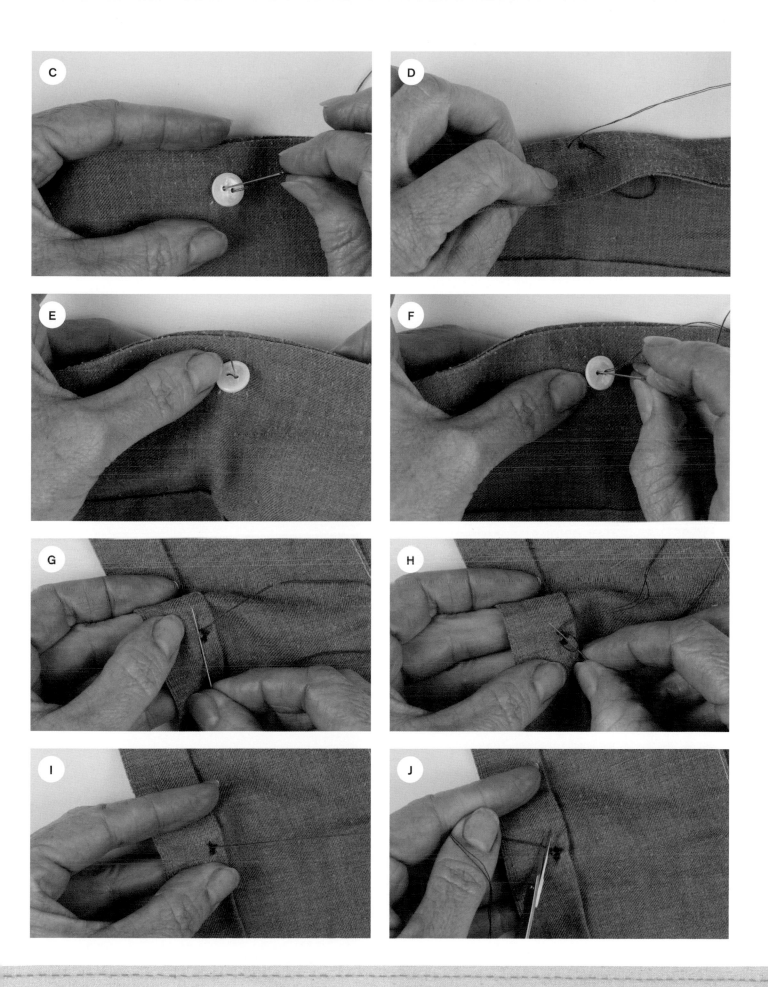

Sewing on a Four-hole Button

Buttons with four holes are most frequently used on men's business shirts. The four holes in the button require additional thread, which makes it a more secure fastener than a button with two holes. Sewing on a button with four holes follows much the same techniques as those for sewing on a two-hole button (see pages 28–9). Once finished, you will have a neat cross of stitches across the centre of the button.

STEP 1

Thread a needle with thread similar in colour to the garment. (The step-by-step photographs show contrasting thread being used, for clarity.) Knot the two strands of thread together (see pages 16–19 for needle-threading and knotting techniques). Refer to the numbering of the holes in the button diagram (top left, opposite page) when working through the following steps.

STEP 2

With one hand, hold the button in place where you want to attach it. Working from the inside of the garment, push the point of the needle through the fabric where the original button had been sewn on and up through hole 1 in the button (**A**).

STEP 3

Pull the needle up and out of the hole in the button and gently pull the thread until the knot is sitting flush with the inside of the fabric. Now take the point of the needle and push it into hole 2 in the button (**B**). Work a diagonal stitch across the face of the button.

STEP 4

On the inside of the garment, pull the needle and thread until the first stitch made on top of the button lies flush and firm. Now make a small stitch to the left and take the needle up through the fabric and into hole 3 in the button (**C**).

You Will Need

- A fine sewing needle
- Thread to match fabric
- Scissors
- A replacement four-hole button (if the original has been lost)

STEP 5

Pull the needle and thread gently until all the excess thread is pulled through hole 3 in the button. Make a diagonal stitch across the face of the button, crossing the original stitch. Now push the needle down and through hole 4 in the button and pull the thread through to the inside of the garment (**D**). You should have made the first 'cross' of stitches across the top of the button (**E**).

STEP 6

Repeat steps 2–5 several times until the button is firmly attached (**F**). Finish off as for the two-hole button (see step 5, page 28).

Tip

To make the button more secure, dip a pin into fabric glue and carefully rub the glue over the knotted threads to prevent them from unravelling. But make sure you don't get glue on the fabric, as it will leave a permanent stain.

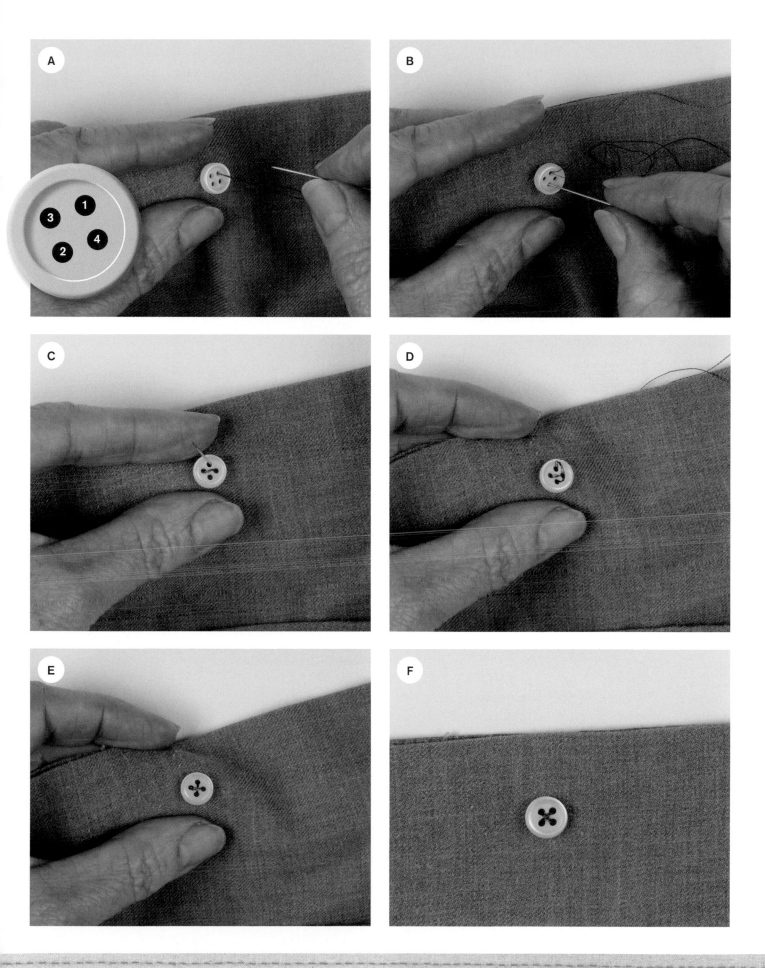

Sewing on a Four-hole Button

Stitching on a Shank Button

Shank buttons are mainly used on jackets and coats. They often have a decorative face with a metal or plastic shank on the back. The button sits slightly up and off the fabric due to the size and depth of the shank. The shank is used to attach the button to the garment.

You Will Need
- Dressmaking chalk
- A fine sewing needle
- Thread to match fabric
- Scissors
- A replacement shank button (if original has been lost)

STEP 1
Using dressmaking chalk, mark the placement for the button (**A**). Thread a needle with some thread matching the colour of the garment. (The step-by-step photographs show contrasting thread being used, for clarity.) Knot the two strands of thread together (see pages 16–19 for needle-threading and knotting techniques).

STEP 2
Take the point of the needle through a few strands of the fabric right on the chalk mark. Pull the thread so that the knot sits flush against the chalk mark (**B**).

STEP 3
Make a small fold in the fabric and hold the button so that the shank is just above the chalk mark and where you have pulled the thread through (**C**).

STEP 4
Hold the button. Pass the needle through the shank, down through the fabric, making a tiny little stitch (**D**). Bring the needle back up through the fabric and through the shank once more. Repeat this sewing action four or five times (**E**). Don't pull the thread too tightly and keep the tension of the thread even. This will ensure that the button has a little bit of movement.

STEP 5
Run the needle along through all the stitches you have made between the shank and the fabric (**F**). Wrap the thread around the base of the stitches three times (**G**). Push the needle right through to the inside of the garment (**H**) and tie off the thread to the inside of the garment, securing it with a neat knot. Snip off any excess thread, close to the original stitching. You will now have a firmly attached and aligned button (**I**).

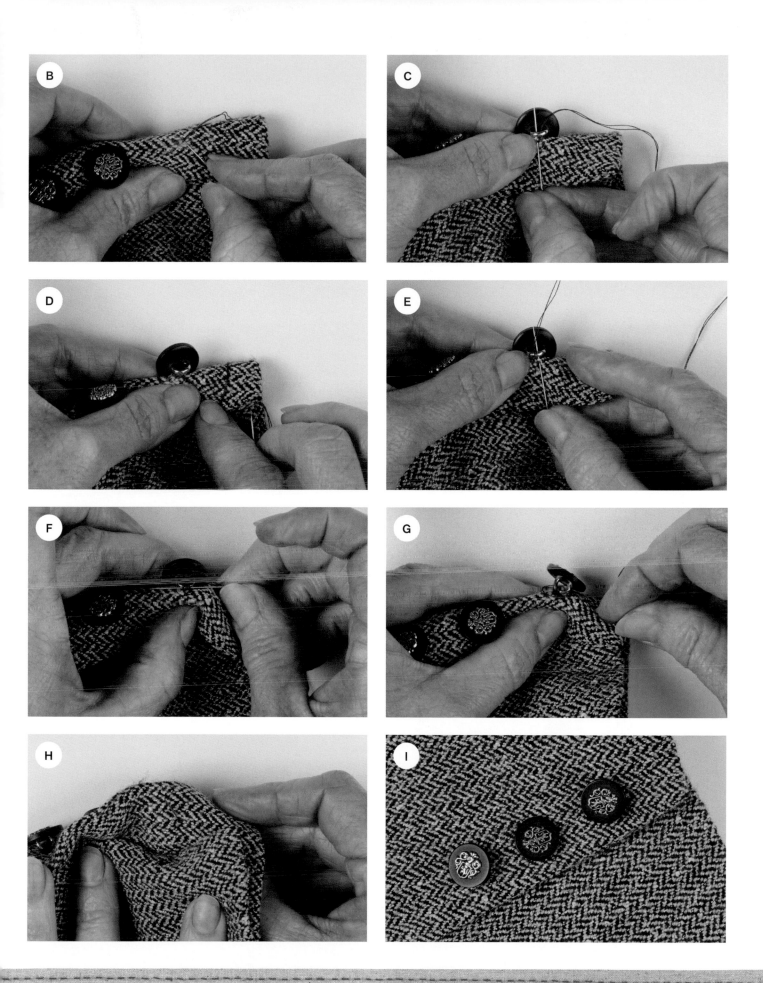

Making a Buttonhole

To make a buttonhole is relatively straightforward. Before marking and cutting the hole, make sure you measure the width and height of the button you wish to use. The buttonhole needs to be approximately ⅛in (3mm) longer than the width of the button for it to slide through easily.

WITH A SEWING MACHINE

If you know how to operate a sewing machine it's very easy to create a professional-looking buttonhole. Most modern sewing machines have a built-in, automatic buttonhole feature and a specific buttonhole foot that either clips or screws on. Refer to your sewing machine's manual to find out if the machine has these features and how to use them. Make sure you use thread that matches the colour of the garment.

You Will Need
- Thread to match fabric
- Needle
- Scissors
- Water-soluble fabric marker pen
- Tape measure

BY HAND
STEP 1

Use a fabric marker pen to mark where the buttonhole should go and cut the fabric. Thread a sharp needle and knot one end of the thread. Working with the right side of the fabric facing up, diagonally insert the needle at the back of the buttonhole, about ⅛in (3mm) from the cut edge of the hole (**A**).

STEP 2

Bring the point of the needle through the fabric into the buttonhole opening. Work from left to right. Slide the thread under the point of the needle. Pull the needle through the fabric. The thread will have formed a small loop, sealing up the raw edge of the buttonhole (**B**).

STEP 3

Continue working stitches around the buttonhole edge (**C**). Place the stitches very close together to make a firm edge (**D**). When finished, secure the thread to the wrong side of the garment.

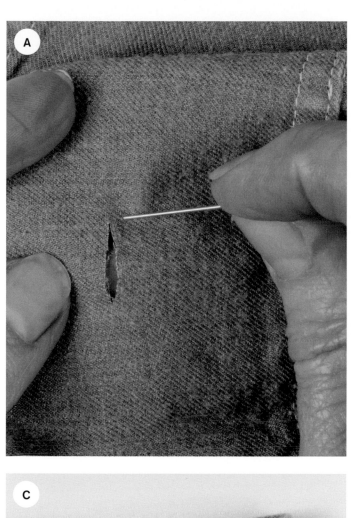

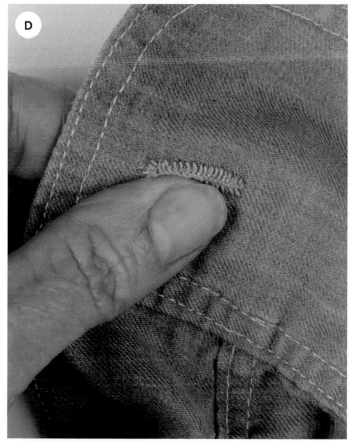

Sewing on Hooks and Eyes

Hooks and eyes are fasteners used to hold the edges of a garment together or to hold fabric together when it is overlapped. They are available in various sizes and colours to match different fabrics. Most hooks and eyes are made from metal for durability but you can also buy plastic fasteners. There are hooks and eyes that are suitable for blouses and dresses and sturdier varieties that are used to secure the waistbands on skirts and trousers (see page 38).

You Will Need
- Needle
- Thread to match fabric
- Water-soluble fabric marker pen
- Scissors
- Hooks and eyes

Most hooks and eyes are sewn in place by hand or with the use of a sewing machine. The no-sew versions must be clamped in place and involve the use of specific tools. These fastenings take more skill to attach to a garment and you should follow the instructions that are included with the package. For edges that just meet, use either straight stitch or buttonhole stitch (see pages 18–21) to attach the hook and eye.

ATTACHING THE HOOK
STEP 1
Thread a needle with thread matching the colour of the garment. (The step-by-step photographs show contrasting thread being used, for clarity.) Knot the two strands of thread together (see pages 16–19 for needle-threading and knotting techniques). Select a hook (and eye) that is suitable for the fabric. Place the hook on the wrong side of the garment about ⅛in (3mm) in from the edge of the finished seam.

STEP 2
Start sewing the hook onto the material with a few stitches. Bring the needle up to the top surface of fabric (**A**), across the bend of the hook and back down to the underside of the fabric. Try to stitch between the two layers of fabric so that the stitches don't show on the outside of the garment.

STEP 3
Sew the hook in place with either straight or buttonhole stitches (**B**). Stitch through the holes all the way around both loops (**C**), then, coming up from the underside, stitch across the end of the hook again to hold it flat (**D**).

ATTACHING THE EYE
STEP 1
Align the sides of the fabric that you wish to fasten together.

STEP 2
Mark the position for the eye with a fabric marker pen, allowing the eye to extend slightly past the finished seam of the garment (**A**).

ATTACHING THE HOOK

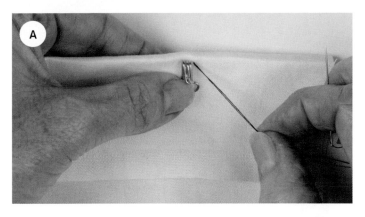

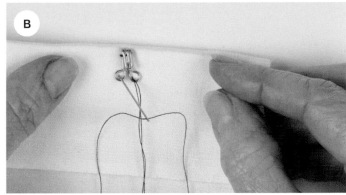

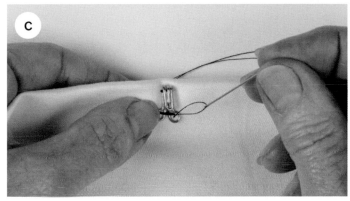

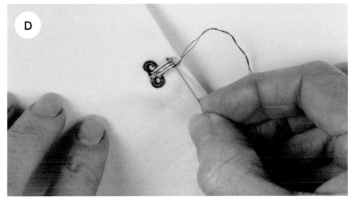

ATTACHING THE EYE

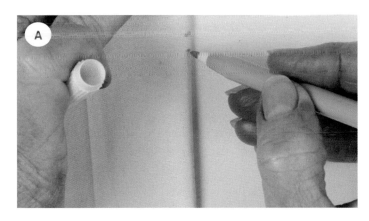

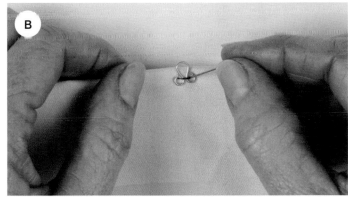

STEP 3

Using either straight or buttonhole stitch, attach the loop to the inside edge of the opposite side of the garment (**B**). Continue stitching through both loops of the eye (**C**), remembering to stitch between the two layers of fabric so that the stitches don't show on the outside of the garment. When the stitching is complete, finish off with a knot and snip off any excess thread.

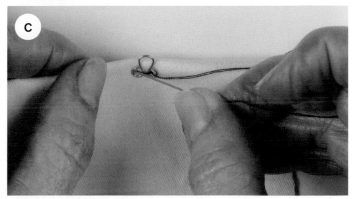

Sewing Metal Hooks and Eyes onto a Waistband

Metal fasteners are very sturdy and are usually used on the waistbands of trousers, skirts and other garments made from medium to heavyweight fabrics. They sit nice and flat on the inside of the waistband.

SEWING THE HOOK ONTO A WAISTBAND

STEP 1
Mark the placement for the hook onto the fabric using a water-soluble fabric marker pen. Thread a needle with matching thread, then make a knot.

STEP 2
Take the point of the needle down one of the holes in the metal hook. Bring it back up through the fabric a small distance away from the edge of the hook. Repeat this stitch several times, sewing in the same entry and exit holes (**A**).

STEP 3
When the stitching feels firm, slide the tip of the needle under the hook, through one layer of fabric and up into the adjacent hole and make several stitches in the same way (**B**). Continue stitching until the hook has been attached securely through all its holes.

STEP 4
Re-thread the needle and tie the ends of the thread into a knot. Slide the point of the needle up and through the hole at the top of the hook catching a few strands of fabric as you work. Bring the needle and thread right through the hole then sew back down into the fabric where you started from. Repeat this stitch a few times and pull the thread so that the stitch sits firmly and neatly. When the stitching is complete, knot off the thread and snip off any excess.

SEWING THE EYE ONTO A WAISTBAND

STEP 1
Overlap the waistband and position the hook onto the fabric where you wish it to connect with the eye. Mark the placement of the eye using a fabric marker pen. Thread a needle and tie the two ends of thread into a knot. Make a few small back stitches on one of the marks on the fabric.

STEP 2
Make a small stitch in the fabric, bringing the needle up and through the metal eye (**A**). Make several little stitches to secure it to the fabric (**B**).

STEP 3
Once the end of the eye feels secure, pass the needle underneath the eye so that you can bring it out to the upper side of the fabric again to attach the other end of the eye (**C**). Repeat step 2 until the eye is firmly stitched in at the other end (**D**) too. When the stitching is complete, knot off the thread and snip off any excess.

You Will Need
- Needle
- Thread
- Hook
- Eye
- Scissors
- Water-soluble fabric marker pen

SEWING THE HOOK ONTO A WAISTBAND

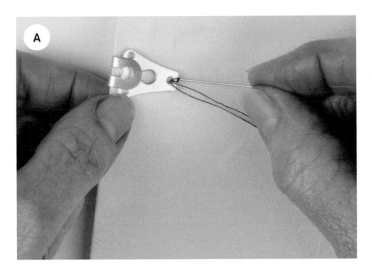

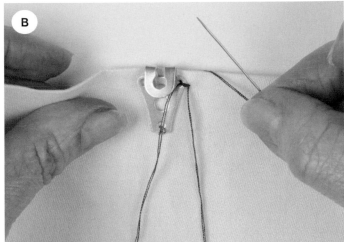

SEWING THE EYE ONTO A WAISTBAND

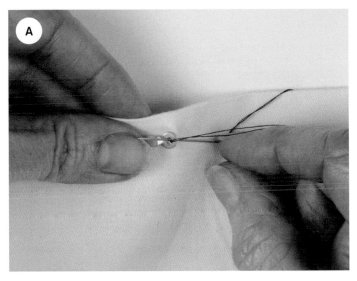

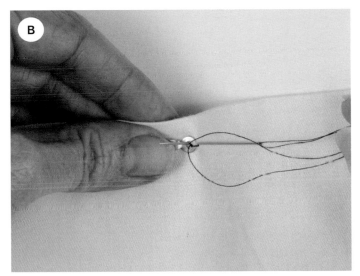

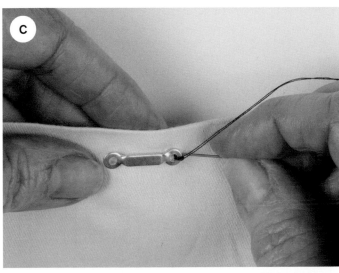

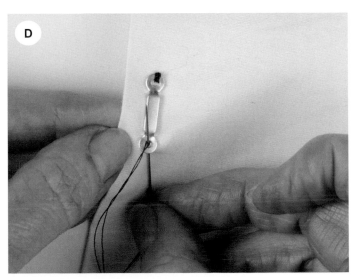

Sewing on Snap Fasteners

Snap fasteners come in several sizes for lightweight to heavyweight fabrics and are available in metal and plastic. They are used to close seams and to secure a closure where there is little strain on the garment, as they are not as strong as hooks and eyes. Snap fasteners come in two parts, the ball snap and socket, each placed on opposite sides of the closure.

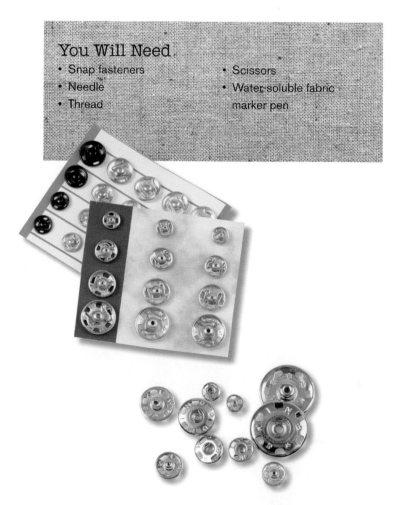

You Will Need
- Snap fasteners
- Needle
- Thread
- Scissors
- Water-soluble fabric marker pen

STEP 1
Mark the placement for the snaps onto your garment using a water-soluble fabric marker pen (**A**). The ball of the snap is usually placed about ⅛in (3mm) from the edge of the fabric if it is being used to close a seam.

STEP 2
Thread a needle with thread that matches the colour of the garment. (The step-by-step photographs show contrasting thread being used, for clarity.) Knot the two strands of thread together (see pages 16–19 for needle-threading and knotting techniques). Take the point of the needle through a few strands of fabric where you wish to attach the snap. Sew a few stitches on top of each other to fasten the thread.

STEP 3
Pass the point of the needle through one hole on the snap. Pull the thread all the way through and take the needle back down an adjacent hole (**B**).

STEP 4
Bring the needle back up in the next hole and continue stitching around the snap until it is securely in place (**C**). Try not to sew right through the top surface fabric as the stitches will show. When finished, knot off the remaining thread and snip off any excess. The socket is attached in exactly the same way on the other side of the closure.

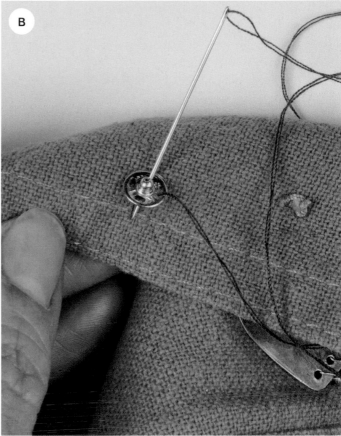

Sewing on Velcro Closures

Velcro is a nylon product that consists of two surfaces which grip when pressed together. One surface has a rough surface made of little hooks while the facing surface has soft loops with a slightly raised pile. When the two layers are pressed together the hooks interlock with the loops. Velcro comes in the form of strips or dots and can be used to close pockets, waistbands and front fly closures, as well to attach a range of other everyday items.

You Will Need
- Tape measure
- Velcro tape
- Scissors
- Needle
- Thread
- Pins
- Sewing machine (optional)

STITCHING VELCRO TO FABRIC

Sew-in hook-and-loop tape (Velcro) is suitable for a variety of different fabrics. It can be machine stitched to a garment using the straight stitch setting. Always close the tape together before laundering to minimize lint build-up.

STEP 1
Use a tape measure to determine what length of tape you require for the opening (**A**). Cut two pieces of tape, 1 x hook and 1 x loop, to the same length.

STEP 2
Position and then pin one piece of the tape to the fabric (**B**).

STEP 3
Thread a needle with thread matching the colour of the tape. (The step-by-step photographs show contrasting thread being used, for clarity.) Knot one end of the thread (see pages 16–19 for needle-threading and knotting techniques). Sew the tape to the fabric (**C**) using straight stitch (see page 18). Try not to stitch all the way through to the other side of the fabric but instead catch just a few strands of fabric when sewing. When the stitching is completed, knot the thread securely and trim off with scissors (**D**).

STEP 4
Attach the second strip of tape in the same way ensuring that, once stitched, the two layers of tape will be aligned and will grip each other firmly, creating a neat closure (**E**).

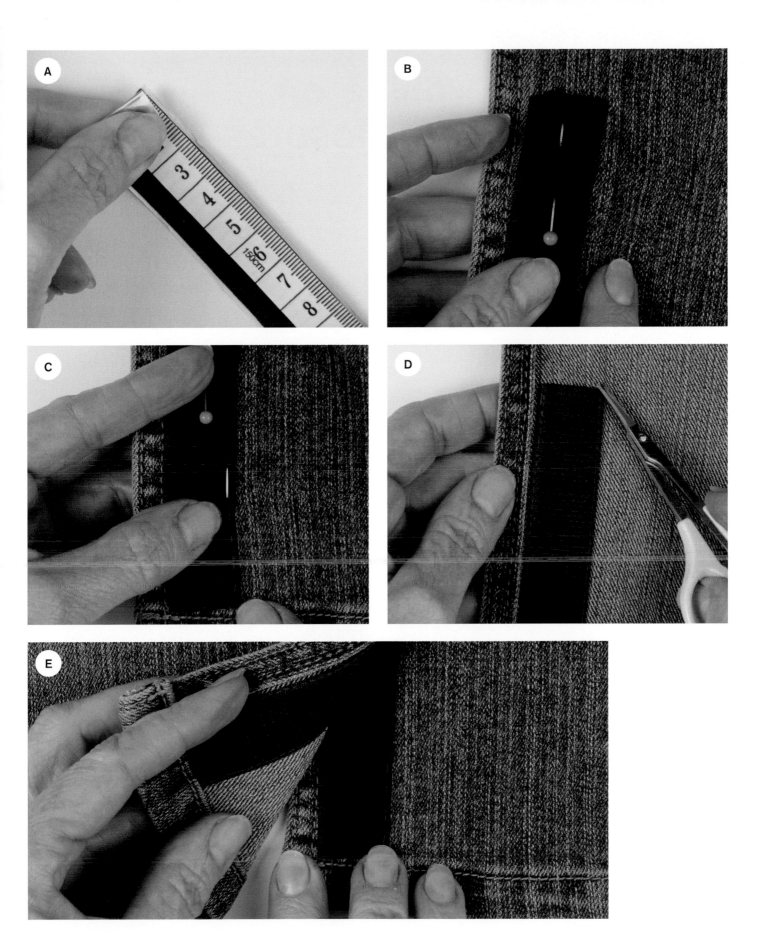

Ironing on Velcro Closures

Iron-on Velcro tape is exactly the same as the sew-on variety (see pages 42–3), except that it has a pre-glued backing, which, when pressed down onto fabric and ironed, adheres to the fabric. It is suitable for use with cotton and linen fabrics, but is not suitable for use on synthetic, polyester, acrylic, wool or silk fabrics as the adhesive, when heated, may damage and distort the fabric.

You Will Need
- Iron-on Velcro dots or strips
- Scissors
- Pins
- Iron
- Handkerchief

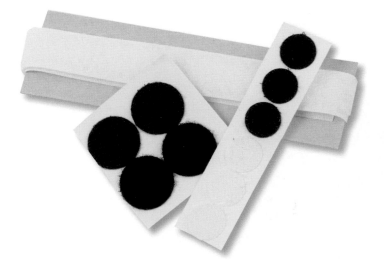

STEP 1
Read the manufacturer's instructions on the package before using the tape. Position the smooth pre-glued side of one piece of the tape down onto the fabric (**A**).

STEP 2
Pin the tape in place so that it won't move when pressed with an iron (**B**).

STEP 3
Turn the fabric over. Place a handkerchief over the fabric to prevent scorching. Set the iron to the correct heat setting as suggested by the packet instructions. Firmly press the iron onto the handkerchief. Hold the iron in place for several seconds (**C**).

STEP 4
Turn the fabric over and try to lift the edge of the tape with a fingernail. If it lifts, press it again until fully bonded to the fabric.

STEP 5
Repeat this procedure for the opposite side, ensuring that the tape is placed in the correct position to align exactly with the piece on the other side of the closure. Once the second piece of tape is attached, wait five minutes before pressing the two layers together.

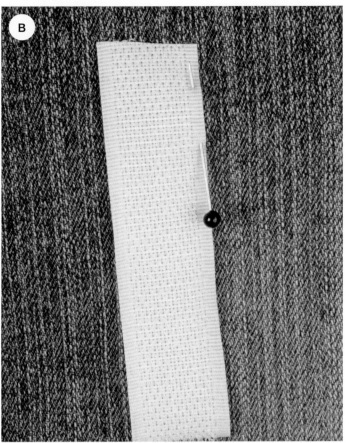

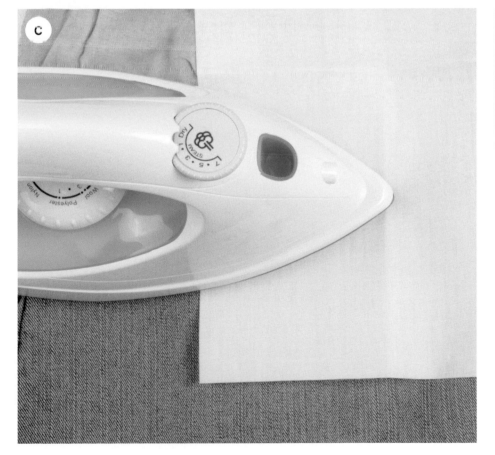

Tip
Never press the iron directly onto the tape as it will damage the surface.

Replacing Metal Snaps

Removing damaged snaps from a garment can be difficult and replacing them is not always that easy. Once the old or damaged snap is removed, it may be necessary to use a snap that is larger than the original so that the prongs of the new snap have some fabric to bite into.

You Will Need
- Packet of metal snaps
- Snap tool
- Butter knife
- Water-soluble fabric marker pen

Tip
Snaps come in a variety of sizes. Keep a small collection in your DIY sewing kit for emergencies, but make sure they are well out of the reach of children as the prongs are very sharp and dangerous if swallowed.

STEP 1
Using a butter knife, slide the blade under the prongs of the snap (**A**) and pry them up out of the fibres of the fabric.

STEP 2
Mark the place for the ball part of the snap on the overlap side of the garment with a marker pen (**B**). Follow the manufacturer's instructions for attaching the snap. You will probably need to use a snap tool (**C**). The ball snap should now be secured neatly in place over the hole of the old ball snap (**D**).

STEP 3
Align the overlap of the closure and mark the place where the socket part of the fastener is to be positioned. Attach the socket part of the snap in the same way. You should now have both the ball-and-socket part of the snap attached to the garment (**E**).

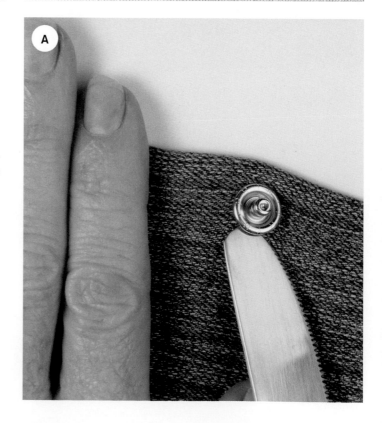

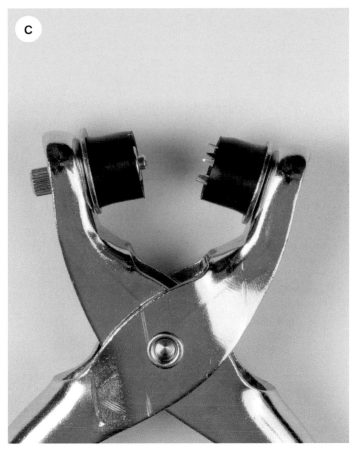

Replacing Metal Snaps

Replacing Metal Eyelets

Eyelets are usually made of a soft metal tube that is shaped by machine to look like a rivet. An eyelet is often used in casual clothing or garments that are secured with laces rather than buttons or zips. Designers insert them into garments to create a fashion statement. They can be both decorative and functional and come in a variety of different sizes and colours.

You Will Need

- Fabric for initial patching (if necessary)
- Water-soluble fabric marker pen
- Scissors
- Eyelet tool or hammer and punch
- Packet of eyelets

Tips

Use eyelet tools when working with lightweight fabrics and a hammer and punch for heavier materials.

Eyelet tools can be expensive. Check out craft shops for inexpensive papercraft which can be used instead.

If you wish to add a decorative finish to a ready-made garment using eyelets, visit your local craft shop. Coloured and fancy eyelets are often used by scrap book hobbyists. You'll find a wide selection on offer in the papercrafts section or online.

STEP 1

If the eyelet in the fabric has been pulled out, patch the inside of the fabric before inserting a new one.

STEP 2

Purchase an eyelet tool and pack of metal eyelets (**A**). Carefully read the instructions on the packet before replacing the eyelet.

STEP 3

Mark the position for the eyelet with a fabric marker pen. Cut a small X-shaped slit where the eyelet will be inserted. Carefully attach the eyelet blank to the lower jaw of the eyelet tool and a pronged eyelet to the upper jaw. Position the tool over the fabric, and squeeze it firmly (**B**). You should now have a new eyelet in place (**C**).

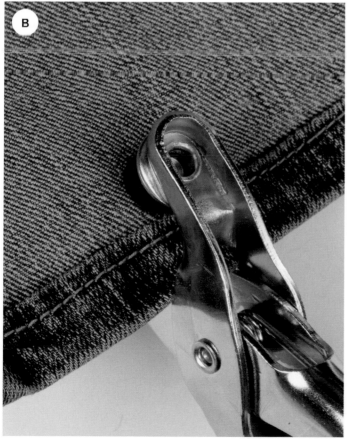

Attaching Buttons and Decorative Studs

There are several stud kits on the market and you should read the instructions on the back of the packaging before starting to attach the stud. These tools hold the stud in place over the outer garment and, when they are hit with a hammer or pressed by hand, the jaws of the tool create enough pressure on the stud to force a hole in the fabric. This allows the stud to penetrate the fabric and seal with the backing tack on the inside of the garment. As the stud and its joining connector link, the metal is pressed together, sealing the stud to the garment.

You Will Need
- Jean studs and applicator (kit)
- Water-soluble fabric marker pen
- Darning needle (if necessary)
- Hammer

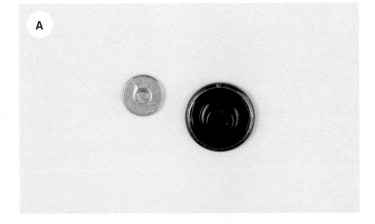

A

STEP 1
Place both the stud and the backing tack (**A**) into the plastic applicator (**B**).

STEP 2
Using a fabric marker pen, mark the position for the new stud.

STEP 3
Position the stud applicator around either side of the fabric, ensuring that the stud is on the outside of the fabric and the backing tack is on the inside (**C**). Hit the applicator firmly with a hammer (**D**) to seal the stud (**E**). If the fabric is very dense, or you are working with several layers of material, make a small hole with a darning needle to assist the securing of the back to the stud.

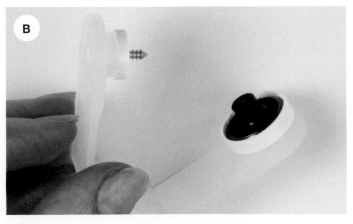

B

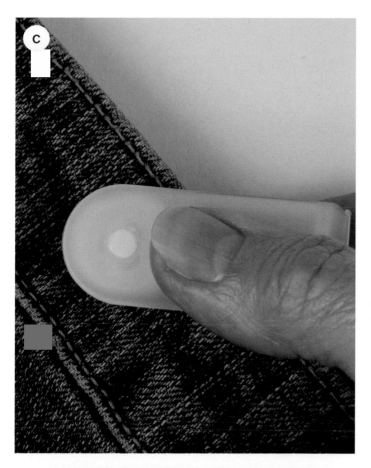

Making Holes in a Leather Belt

Most of us probably own a few trusted, good-quality leather belts that have become firm favourites to wear with trousers – whether casual jeans or formal business suits. But, over the years, most of us have also probably noticed our waistlines fluctuating! Whether you've been on a successful diet or gained a few pounds, it's very easy to punch in some new holes.

You Will Need
- Hole punch
- Dressmaking chalk

Tip
If the leather is thick, make a small hole with a darning needle to help the jaws of the punch penetrate the belt.

STEP 1
Using a dressmaker's chalk pencil, mark on the inside of the belt where the desired hole is to be made (**A**), making sure it is in the mid-line of the belt. To achieve a perfectly symmetrical and invisible finish you should ideally make any new holes the same distance apart as the existing holes on the belt (too many holes too close together may weaken the belt and cause it to twist). But if you are making just one extra hole, don't worry if it is a bit closer to any existing holes.

STEP 2
Turn the head of the leather punch tool so that the correct size punch is sitting opposite the base of the pliers.

STEP 3
Place the leather into the jaws of the punch tool. Place the tip of the punch over the mark for the new hole (**B**).

STEP 4
Grip the handles very firmly and squeeze tightly. A neat hole will be created. Remove the belt from the jaws (**C**).

Seams

Mending a Seam

Often the seams on skirts or trousers weaken over a period of time due to stress on that section of stitching. When threads break and stitches unravel, thread a needle and repair it quickly and easily using this strong and easy-to-master stitch. Always practise on a scrap of fabric if you haven't sewn before. Once your stitches are neat and regular, you're ready to make the DIY repair.

You Will Need
- Needle
- Thread
- Scissors
- Pins
- Iron and pressing cloth

STEP 1
Seams can weaken and come open on any garment (**A**). Pin the open seam together. Thread a needle with thread to match your garment. Tie a double knot joining the two ends together. Make a neat stitch in the fabric to secure the thread (**B**).

STEP 2
Make a small straight stitch. Make a second stitch and as the needle comes up and out of the fabric, pass the needle point down the exit hole of the first stitch (**C**).

STEP 3
Make another stitch, keeping the spacing of the stitches even. Back-stitch (see page 22) into the exit of the second stitch. Continue sewing until the seam is repaired. Knot off the thread and trim off any excess (**D**).

STEP 4
Press the seam flat with a warm iron and pressing cloth (**E**).

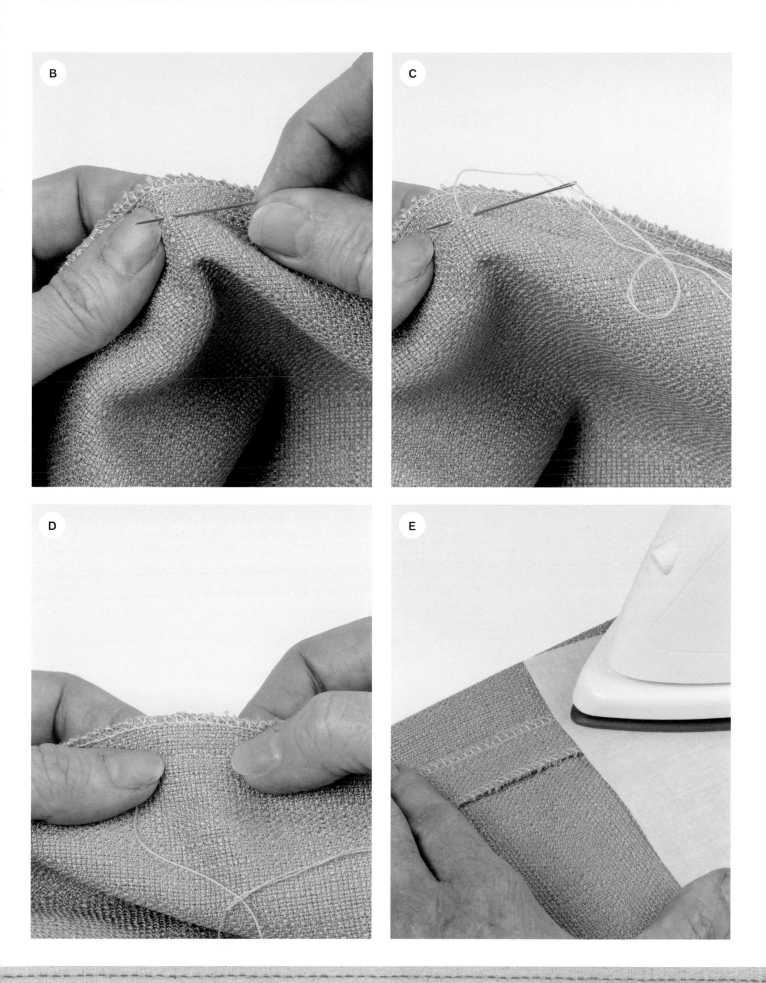

Taking in a Seam

Have you been on a successful diet and now all your clothes are too big? Or is a staple piece of your wardrobe now just a bit too loose in one place? Not all such clothes need to go to the charity shop, especially those favourite or designer pieces that you know you look fabulous in. Instead, you can simply take in a few seams and extend their lifespan.

You Will Need
- Pins
- Water-soluble fabric marker pen
- Needle
- Thread
- Scissors
- Sewing machine (if using)
- Iron and pressing cloth

STEP 1
Turn the garment inside out and put it on. Pinch the excess fabric with one hand and pin it (it can be helpful to have someone else do this for you). Carefully remove the garment and then straighten up the pins, adding a few more if necessary (**A**).

STEP 2
Turn the garment right side out and try it on again to double check that the alteration is correct and not too tight or still too loose – adjust the pins if necessary. Turn the garment inside out once more and mark a stitching line with a fabric marker pen, following the placement of the pins (**B**).

STEP 3
If sewing by hand, thread a needle with thread matching the colour of the garment. Knot one end of the thread (see pages 16–19 for needle-threading and knotting techniques). Sew down the new seam line using small, neat back stitches (see page 22). If using a sewing machine, set it on straight stitch with a small stitch length and sew along the marked line, removing the pins as you go (**C**). Back-stitch when you start and finish to secure the thread. Knot off the threads when the stitching is completed and trim off excess.

STEP 4
Press the new seam with a warm iron. If the fabric is particularly bulky, open up the old seam with embroidery scissors or a seam ripper, and iron between the two flaps of fabric so that they can lie flat. Alternatively, if you're confident you won't need to let the garment out again, you could trim off some of the now-increased seam allowance, but be careful to still leave a seam allowance of at least ⅜in (1cm). Turn the garment right side out and iron the new seam again, placing a clean handkerchief between the iron and the garment to help protect delicate fabrics from scorching (**D**).

Letting Out a Seam

Letting out a seam is not a big deal as long as there is sufficient fabric inside the stitched seam to let out! Some ready-made garments have been stitched together with an overlocker sewing machine, which cuts off the seam allowance, overcasts the raw edges and stitches the seam together all at the same time. If a garment has no seam allowance, then it's time to pass it on to a friend or charity shop, as trying to make it larger is too time-consuming.

STEP 1
Turn the garment inside out. With a water-soluble fabric marker pen, mark on the seam line where you wish to let out the seam (**A**).

STEP 2
Unpick the seam with a seam ripper or the point of embroidery scissors (**B**) and (**C**).

STEP 3
If sewing by hand, thread a needle with thread matching the colour of the garment. Knot one end of the thread (see pages 16–19 for needle-threading and knotting techniques). Stitch the seam together using small, neat back stitches (see page 22). If using a sewing machine, set it on straight stitch with a small stitch length, and sew along the marked line (**D**). When you have completed the stitching, fasten off the threads and trim down close to the last few stitches.

STEP 4
With the garment still inside out, slightly dampen the seam with a mist of water or place a damp handkerchief over the seam allowance. Press the fabric with a warm dry iron (**E**) to remove the old stitching marks and to open out the seam.

You Will Need
- Water-soluble fabric marker pen
- Ruler
- Seam ripper
- Needle and thread or sewing machine
- Scissors
- Iron and pressing cloth

Repairing a Split Seam in the Crotch of Trousers

The seams in the crotch of trousers often split simply through the friction of daily wear and tear or because they were originally sewn with a poor-quality thread. But don't worry: this is easy to repair by hand or machine, so you can keep those favourite old trousers going a good while longer.

You Will Need
- Needle and thread or sewing machine
- Pins
- Scissors
- Bias binding

STEP 1
Seams in the crotch of trousers are often the first to wear out (**A**). Turn the trousers inside out and pin the split seam of the crotch together (**B**). If sewing by hand, thread a needle with thread similar in colour to the garment. (The step-by-step photographs show contrasting thread being used, for clarity.) Knot the two strands of thread together (see pages 16–19 for needle-threading and knotting techniques). If using a sewing machine, set it on straight stitch with a small stitch length.

STEP 2
Secure the thread at the end of the split seam. Back-stitch over at least 1in (2.5cm) of the machine stitching before the split (**C**). Now sew along the original stitching line using small, neat, even stitches.

STEP 3
Stitch past the split and continue to sew along the machine stitching on the trouser seam for a further 1in (2.5cm) before knotting off the thread (**D**). Snip off excess threads.

STEP 4
To reinforce the seam of the crotch, cut a length of bias binding and pin it over the repair (**E**).

STEP 5
Sew the bias binding over the crotch seam (**F**). If sewing by hand, use straight stitch. Use a narrow zigzag stitch if you are sewing by machine. Set the machine stitch to a small width and length.

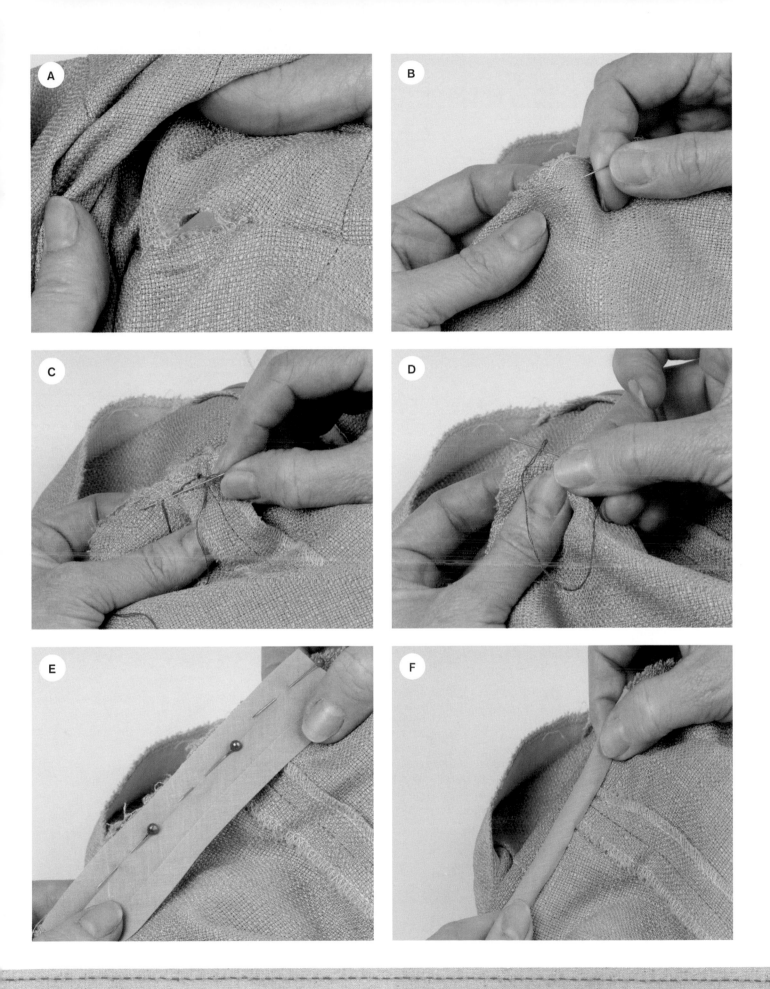

Repairing a Split Seam in Stretch Fabric

Stretch fabric is very different from woven fabric. It has a completely different weave and is made from either synthetic or natural fibres mixed with Lycra or spandex so that, once woven together, the fabric stretches. Just how much the stitches will stretch is determined by how wide the stitches are and the distance between them.

You Will Need
- Needle
- Matching thread
- Sewing machine (optional)
- Scissors

Stretch fabric is often used in leisure and fitness clothing, and as such the seams are often put under extra movement and strain. Thus it is a common problem for the seams in your jogging pants, for example, to split open (**A**).

SEWING STRETCH FABRIC BY HAND
STEP 1
Thread a needle with thread similar in colour to the garment. (The step-by-step photographs show contrasting thread being used, for clarity.) Knot the two strands of thread together.

STEP 2
Back-stitch (see page 22) to start, then stitch along the original machine stitching 1in (2.5cm) before the split occurs. Sew neat little zigzag stitches (see page 24), keeping them evenly spaced and fairly close together (**B**). Stitch past the split and back over another 1in (2.5cm) of machine stitching before knotting the thread and snipping it off with scissors.

SEWING STRETCH FABRIC BY MACHINE
STEP 1
Set the sewing machine to zigzag, with a small stitch width and length. Back-stitch over a small section of stitches before the split and continue to sew along the original stitching line, sewing the seam back together (**C**), and continue another 1in (2.5cm) past the end of the split.

STEP 2
Back-stitch to secure the thread at the end of your sewing. Remove the garment from the machine and trim off the excess threads with scissors.

Hems

Using Iron-on Hemming Web

You don't even need to learn how to sew in order to fix a hem. Hemming tape or web is sold in supermarkets and craft shops and comes in a variety of different widths. The web is a fine layer of heat-sensitive glue. When placed between two layers of material and heated with an iron the web melts, sticking the two layers of fabric together.

You Will Need
- Roll of hemming web
- Scissors
- Iron
- Handkerchief or pressing cloth
- Tape measure

STEP 1
Measure the length of hem that needs to be repaired using a tape measure (**A**).

STEP 2
Cut the required length of hemming web (**B**).

STEP 3
Slide the web under the free edge of the hem and position it so that it is concealed by the fabric (**C**).

STEP 4
Place a slightly damp handkerchief or clean piece of fabric over the hem and press with a warm iron (**D**). Allow the hem to cool completely before wearing or laundering the garment.

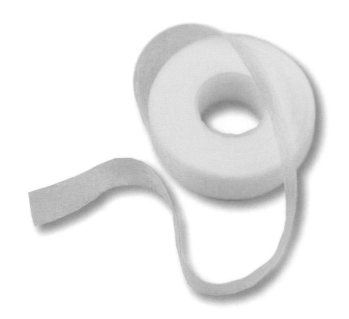

Tips
Ironing the repaired hem through a handkerchief or cloth will help to prevent scorching, and if any webbing becomes dislodged it will stick to the cloth, not the iron.

If the web does come into direct contact with the face of the iron it will melt on to it and you'll have a sticky black mess that's difficult to get off!

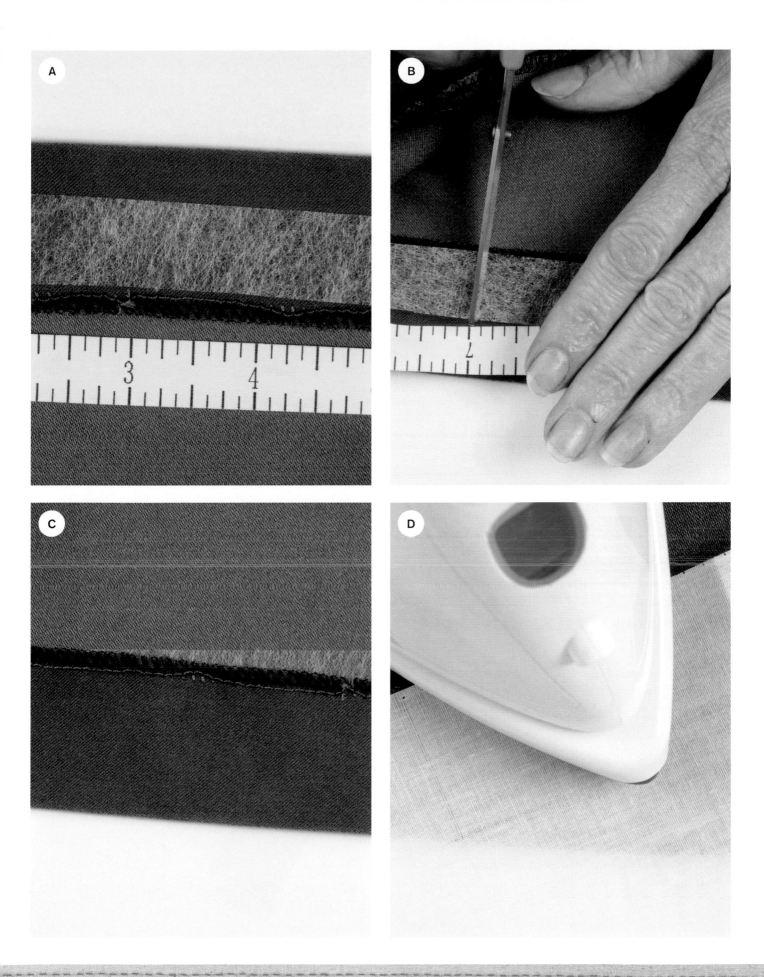

Repairing a Hem

Herringbone stitch is the ideal stitch for repairing the hem on a skirt or trousers. It may take a little longer to sew than the simple slip stitch (see page 20), but it creates a secure neat finish that is well worth the effort when mending quality clothing. Before starting your repair, you may wish to practise the stitch by reviewing the step-by-step technique demonstrated on page 22.

You Will Need
- Pins
- Needle
- Matching thread
- Scissors

STEP 1
Carefully secure the threads of the unravelled hem. Thread a needle and back-stitch (see page 22) the threads to the edge of the hem to secure them in place. Trim off any excess thread.

STEP 2
Pin the unravelled hem in place (**A**). Thread a needle and tie a knot in one end of the thread. Back-stitch into the hem edge to secure the thread (**B**).

STEP 3
Make a long, diagonal stitch from left to right across the free edge of the hem fold and back through the flat fabric of the garment, about ¼in (6mm) from the hem edge (**C**).

STEP 4
With the needle pointing to the left, make a small stitch in the fabric. Pierce the fabric with the point of the needle sewing from right to left (**D**).

STEP 5
Bring the needle out of the hem and make another long, diagonal stitch from left to right so that the threads cross (**E**). The stitches should be evenly spaced and approximately the same size (**F**).

STEP 6
When the stitching is complete, finish off by back-stitching in the edge of the folded hem fabric before cutting the excess thread with scissors.

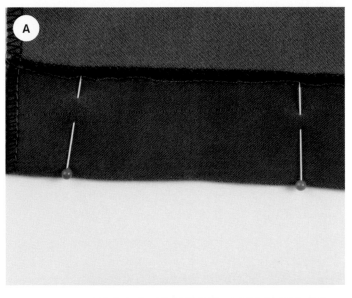

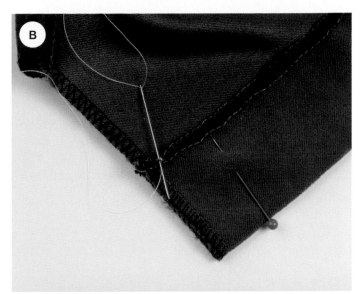

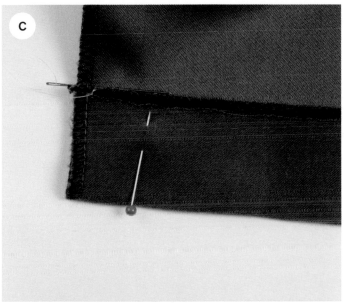

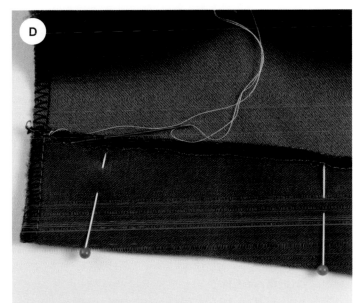

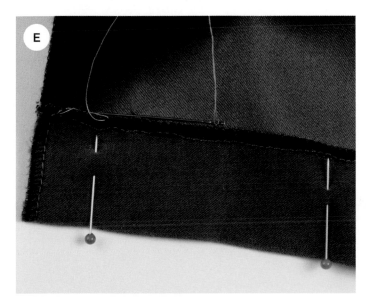

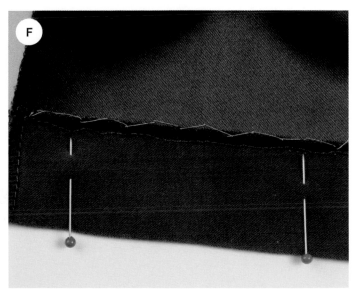

Invisible Hems

This is a particularly handy technique for hemming fabric such as silk or linen where you wish the hemming stitches to be as unobtrusive on the right side of the fabric as possible. In the step-by-step photographs, right, a contrasting pink thread has been used, as opposed to transparent thread, for clarity.

You Will Need
- Tape measure
- Interfacing
- Water soluble-fabric marker pen (optional) and ruler
- Iron
- Pins
- Handkerchief or pressing cloth
- Fine needle
- Transparent nylon thread

STEP 1
Measure and cut out a piece of interfacing to the width and length of the hem to be repaired. Mark the outline of the piece with a fabric marker pen if this helps (**A**).

STEP 2
Place the piece of interfacing over the opened-up area of hem, i.e. onto the wrong side of the fabric (**B**). Place a handkerchief or clean piece of fabric over the top and press, working along the very edge of the fabric of the hem.

STEP 3
Measure the depth of the intended hem and pin the hem up into position (**C**). Press the fold of the hem lightly with an iron (**D**).

STEP 4
Using transparent thread, sew the folded edge of the hem to the flat interfaced fabric of the garment (**E**) using slip stitch (see page 20) or herringbone stitch (see page 22). Knot off the ends of the thread securely when the sewing is completed.

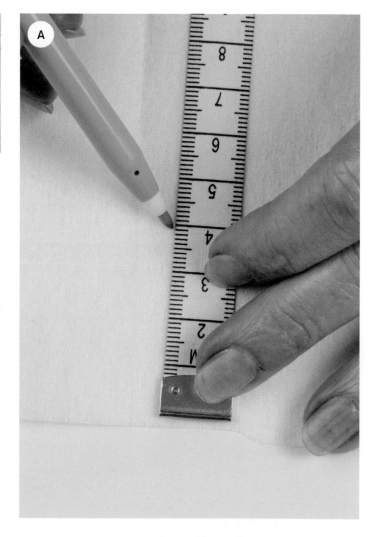

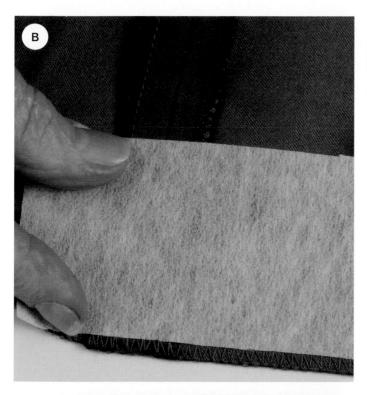

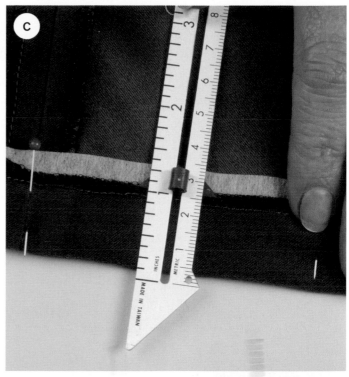

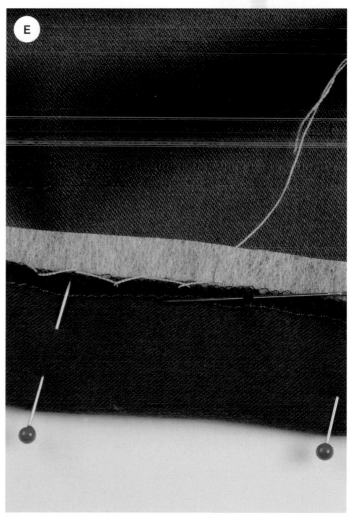

Hemming with Slip Stitch

Slip stitch is a fast, easy stitch to master and is ideal for quickly repairing or taking up hems on clothing, curtains and many other home furnishings. Before commencing your repair, you may wish to practise doing slip stitch by reviewing the step-by-step technique demonstrated on page 20.

You Will Need
- Pins
- Needle
- Matching thread
- Scissors

STEP 1
Secure the threads of the unravelled hem. Thread a needle and back-stitch (see page 22) the threads to the edge of the hem to secure them in place. Trim off any excess thread with scissors. Pin the hem to be stitched in place (**A**).

STEP 2
Work from right to left. Thread a needle with a long strand of thread that is colour-matched to the fabric. (The step-by-step photographs show contrasting thread being used, for clarity.) Knot only one end of the thread. Make a little back stitch in the edge of the hem to secure the knot (**B**).

STEP 3
With the very tip of the needle pick up a few threads of the inside of the garment (i.e. not the hem itself) just level with the edge of the hem (**C**).

STEP 4
Pull the needle until all the thread has been pulled through the strands of fabric.

STEP 5
Push the needle into the edge of the hem, making a small stitch. Slide it along and bring it up and out of the hem, close to the edge of the hem fabric (**D**).

STEP 6
Repeat steps 3–5 and continue to stitch (**E**) until you reach the original stitching. Back-stitch over the original stitching to secure the thread and trim off the excess with scissors.

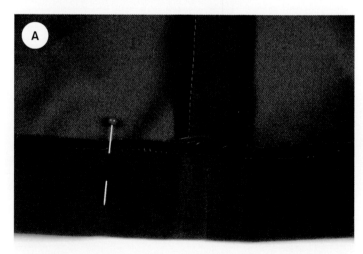

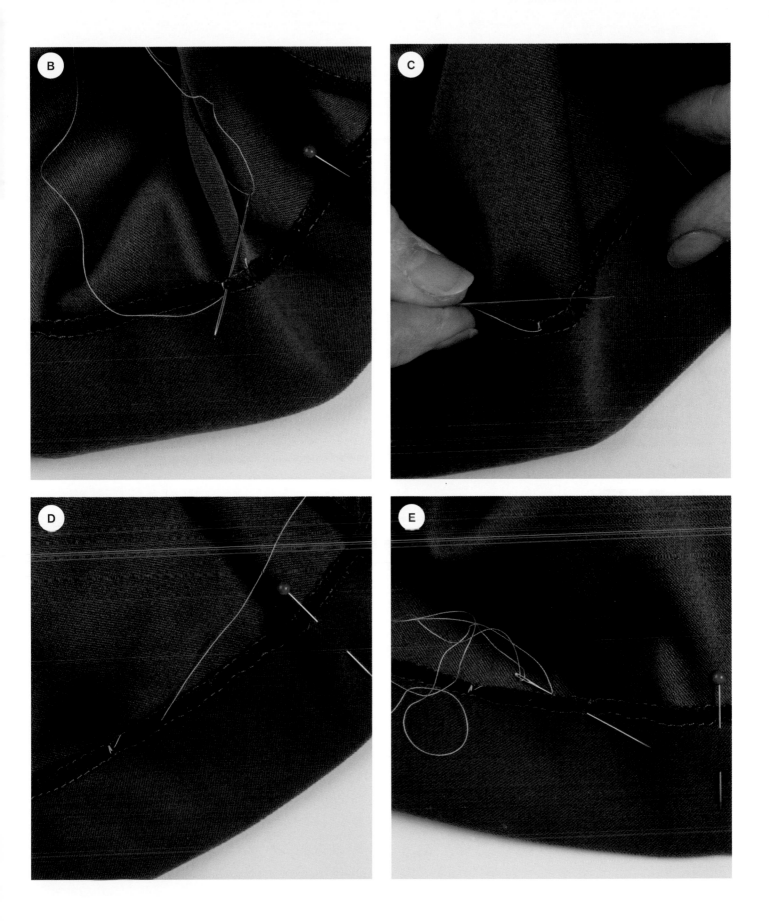

Top-stitching a Hem

Top stitching is used on denim to finish the hems and to add designer detail to the seams. It is also used as a decorative finish in tailoring and for high street fashions. Top-stitching thread is heavier and thicker than regular sewing threads. It is usually a different colour to the fabric as the stitches are intended to be visible.

You Will Need
- Sewing machine
- Jeans needle
- Top-stitching thread
- Pins
- Scissors
- Water-soluble fabric marker pen
- Ruler or measuring gauge

To prevent the thread from fraying as it feeds through the metal eye of the needle and into the fabric, it is important that you use the correct needle. A jeans needle, size 100, will stitch most top-stitching threads.

STEP 1
Top stitching can be used decoratively (**A**) and uses a heavier thread than normal (**B**). Thread the sewing machine with top-stitching thread (**C**) and set it for straight stitch. If there is a top-stitching pattern in your machine's stitch memory, selecting this will ensure that the machine sews the desired stitch.

STEP 2
Pin the hem or seam of the fabric you wish to topstitch. Mark a sewing line with a fabric marker pen (**D**).

STEP 3
Sew on the right side of the fabric (**E**), as this is the visible side (**F**).

STEP 4
When the stitching is completed, back-stitch over a few stitches to secure the thread, remove the fabric from the machine, and trim off the cotton end (**G**). Press the stitching with a warm iron.

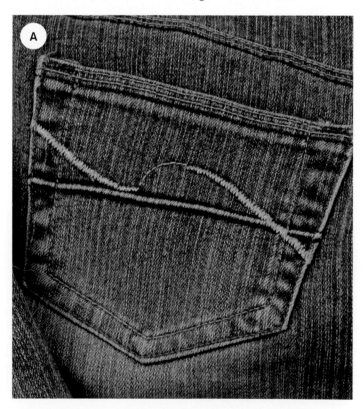

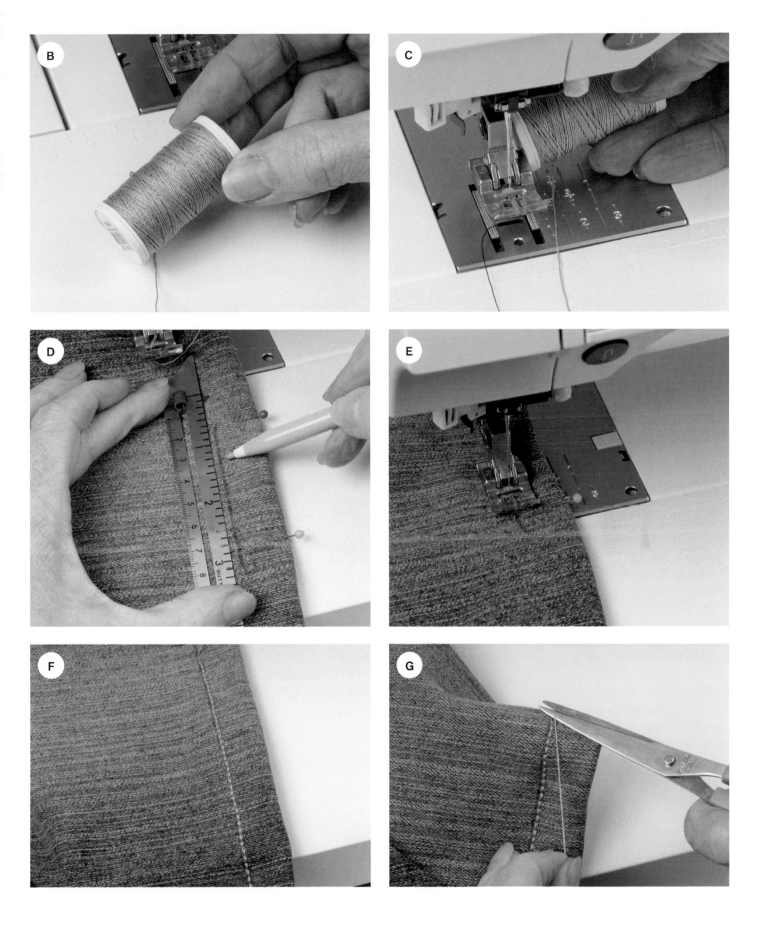

Blind-stitching a Hem

A blind stitch hem is ideal for medium-to-heavyweight fabrics. Most modern sewing machines have this stitch built into their stitch memory. It consists of several small straight stitches followed by one zigzag stitch that jumps to the left. The jump stitch catches the fold of the hem fabric as the machine sews.

You Will Need
- Sewing machine and blind hemming foot
- Transparent thread
- Iron
- Handkerchief or pressing cloth
- Pins

STEP 1
Fold the hem up to the desired depth. Fold the hem back on itself approximately ¼in (6mm) so that the finished edge of the hem is to the right of the fold. Pin in place (**A**).

STEP 2
If you have the sewing machine manual for your machine read the instructions before starting to sew. Attach the blind hem foot and thread the machine with matching thread or transparent thread. (The step-by-step photographs show contrasting thread being used, for clarity.)

STEP 3
As you stitch, the metal guard on the foot should run parallel with the fold of the fabric (**B**). The straight stitch will sew onto the finished edge of the hem and the jump stitch will catch a few fibres of the fold (**C**). Back-stitch to secure the threads when finished.

STEP 4
When the stitching is completed remove the fabric from the machine. Trim off the excess thread. Turn the fabric right side over (**D**) and place a handkerchief or pressing cloth over the stitches but not over the folded edge of the hem. Press the stitches with a warm iron. Do not press the fold of the hem if you are sewing a garment as a blind hem should roll softly and have a rounded finish.

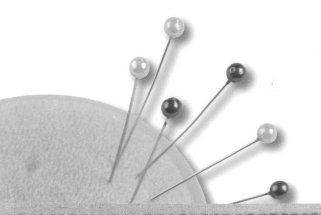

Making a Jumped Hem

This is a couture technique often used on lined garments, such as ballgowns or wedding gowns. However, if you have a lined, ready-made skirt from which you wish to remove any trace of stitching at the hemline then it is possible to sew the free edge of the hem to the lining fabric so that no stitching is seen on the hem of the outer garment. This is ideal when working with heavyweight silks on which, no matter how carefully you sew, the stitching shows on the outer fabric.

You Will Need

- Seam ripper
- Pins
- Scissors
- Pressing cloth
- Iron
- Sewing machine
- Matching thread

STEP 1
Unpick about 12in (30cm) of a side seam in the lining fabric (**A**).

STEP 2
Carefully unpick the hem with a seam ripper or needle (**B**).

STEP 3
Turn the garment inside out so that the right side of the lining hem and of the garment hem are touching.

STEP 4
Stitch the edges of the hems together, sewing all around the hem and back-stitching to secure the threads (**C**).

STEP 5
Turn the skirt right side out through the opening made in the side seam of the lining. Slip-stitch the opening in the lining closed (**D**).

STEP 6
Press the inside of the garment where the two hems have been joined (**E**). Place a pressing cloth over the fold in the hem and press gently with a warm iron. The stitches will be invisible from the outside of the garment (**F**).

Letting Down a Hem

Letting down a hem on a skirt or a pair of trousers is only possible where the present hem has been turned up with a good hem allowance – in other words, there is some 'spare' fabric to 'let down'. Many cheaper, mass-produced garments are not made with this in mind and have the smallest of hems.

You Will Need

- Water-spray bottle
- 3fl oz (75ml) distilled water
- ¾fl oz (20ml) white vinegar
- Handkerchief or pressing cloth
- Pins
- Seam ripper or embroidery scissors
- Iron
- Needle
- Matching thread
- Bias binding (if required)

STEP 1

Unpick the hem using a seam ripper or the point of sharp embroidery scissors (**A**).

STEP 2

Fill a water-spray bottle with 3fl oz (75ml) of distilled water. Add ¾fl oz (20ml) of white vinegar. Shake well then spray the hem fabric and the original fold with the solution (**B**). *NB: Do not spray pure silk or dry-clean-only fabrics.* The vinegar helps to remove creases in woven fabrics. Cover the hem with a handkerchief or clean piece of fabric and press to make it smooth and flat.
If you are only letting down a small amount of the hem allowance, then you will conclude with step 3. If you require the full hem allowance to extend the length of your garment, however, then you will need to sew a strip of bias binding to the lower edge of the hem. To do this, after step 2 (above) follow the alternative step 3, followed by steps 4 and 5.

STEP 3

Measure and then pin the hem to the desired length (**C**). Press the fold of the hem with a warm iron. Sew the hem back into place using either slip stitch (see page 20) or herringbone stitch (see page 22).

STEP 3 ALTERNATIVE

Open one folded edge of the bias binding and pin the bias to the free edge of the hem with right sides of fabrics touching (**D**).

STEP 4

Stitch the bias to the edge of the hem using straight stitch by hand or by machine-sewing in the crease of the bias fold (**E**). The seam allowance will be approximately ¼in (6mm).

STEP 5

The bias binding is now the hem of the garment. Turn up the bias to the inside of the garment. Press the hem flat with a warm iron, pin it into position (**F**) and then slip-stitch it to the garment to secure it in place.

Taking up a Hem

Too often garments are discarded because they are too long. With fashion trends changing from season to season, hems go up and hems go down. With a little time and effort you can shorten the length of the hem of a skirt, dress or pair of trousers following this simple procedure.

You Will Need
- Iron
- Needle
- Matching thread
- Dressmaking chalk or water-soluble fabric-marker pen
- Tape measure or measuring gauge
- Scissors
- Pins

The best method of measuring to alter the hem of a garment is to put the garment on and ask a friend to mark the new hemline for you with chalk or by pinning all around. Short of a helping hand, have a look in a mirror while wearing the garment and make a pen or chalk mark on the garment where you want the new length to be. Take the garment off, measure up from the hemline to this mark and measure and mark a new hemline all around the item of clothing.

STEP 1
Unpick the stitching along the original hem.

STEP 2
Now measure down approximately 2in (5cm) from the mark where you wish the new hem to finish and mark the fabric where the excess hem needs to be cut off (**A**). Mark all around the garment so that you have a clear line on which to cut and remove the excess material. Cut off the excess fabric.

STEP 3
Fold under approx ½in (1cm) of the cut edge of the new hemline. Press the fold down with a warm iron. Turn the hem up to the new hemline marking and pin the hem evenly in place (**B**).

STEP 4
Using slip stitch or herringbone stitch (see pages 20 and 22), sew the fold of the hem fabric to the inside of the garment (**C**). Press the fold of the hem when the stitching is completed.

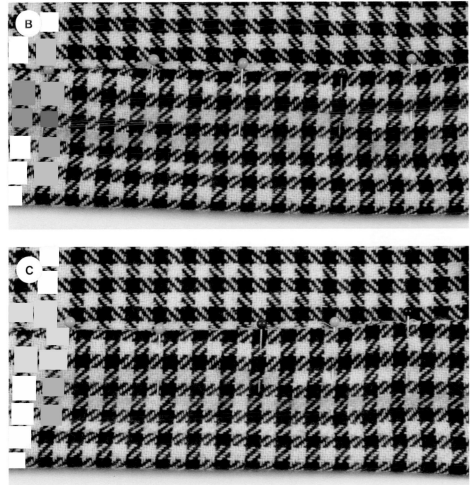

Hemming Stretch Fabric

Hemming stretch fabric by hand is inadvisable, as the stitching needs to be able to stretch with the fabric. If you must hem by hand, sew the garment with a narrow zigzag stitch on the inside using a polyester thread.

You Will Need
- Sewing machine
- Twin needle
- 2 rolls of sewing thread
- Scissors
- Pins
- Water-soluble fabric-marker pen

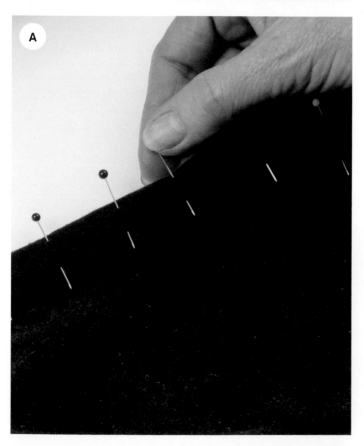

STEP 1
Pin the hem of the fabric to the inside of the garment (**A**). Turn the garment over so that the right side is facing up. If you are unsure of where the end of the hem is now, draw a sewing line along the top surface of the fabric. This line will now be directly over the raw edge of the hem that has been pinned up.

STEP 2
Attach the twin needle (**B**) to the machine. Thread the machine with both rolls of sewing thread and thread each eye of the needle separately with one strand of thread (**C**). Two different coloured threads are shown in the photographs, for clarity.

STEP 3
Set your sewing machine to straight stitch with a small to medium length. If you have drawn a sewing line on the top surface of the fabric (not shown in photo), line up the needles over the top of this line. The needles should be stitching over the raw edge of the hem on the inside of the garment (**D**).

STEP 4
The needles sew a straight stitch on the right side of the material (**E**) but if you look at the inside of the garment you will see that the under-stitching is a zigzag stitch that stretches (**F**).

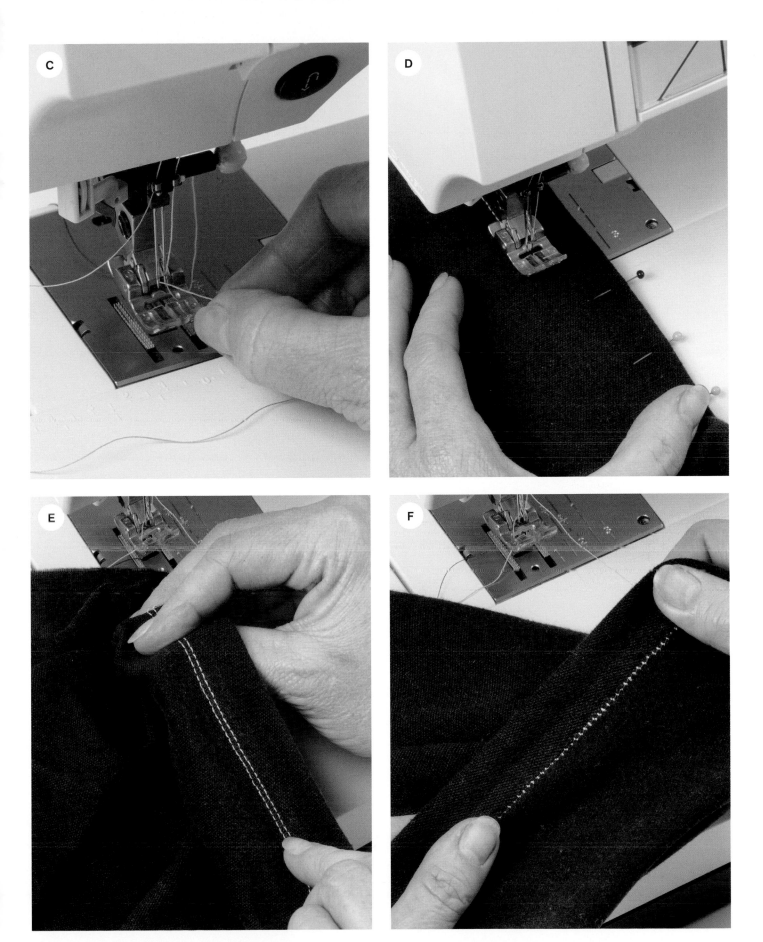

Fix and Repair

Instant Fixes

What do you do when you're at work and the hem of your dress or trouser leg comes down? If you have no sewing kit to hand and it really is a crisis, then you can reach for the office stapler. Another instant fix is double-sided sticky tape. Glue, safety pins, even bulldog clips, can have their uses. There are also many instant fixes that you can buy from the supermarket in your lunch hour.

THE OFFICE STAPLER

While this tool can be a lifesaver, think twice before using it on silk or expensive garments as the staple may cut permanent holes into the fabric.

STEP 1

To prevent the fabric from pinching up into an ugly pucker, place a thin layer of paper between the two folds of material. The paper will act as a stabilizer and give the stapler something to grip. If it's a truly manic moment then forget about the paper and just staple the hem back into place.

STEP 2

Then click, click, click … and now you are fixed.

DOUBLE-SIDED STICKY TAPE

When buttons pop off or hems drop, double-sided sticky tape is
so useful. It works especially well with light or semi-sheer fabrics,
as it is thin and transparent. The steps below show how to fix
a dropped hem.

STEP 1

Cut the desired length of double-sided tape
with scissors. Position the tape and press
the sticky side face down onto the inside
of the fabric.

STEP 2

Peel off the backing paper to expose the
other pre-glued side.

STEP 3

Fold the hem back over and press the edge
down onto the tape. Press from the middle
outwards towards each end of the tape.

STEP 4

As you can see, there are no marks or
holes, and the hem has been instantly
(albeit temporarily) fixed.

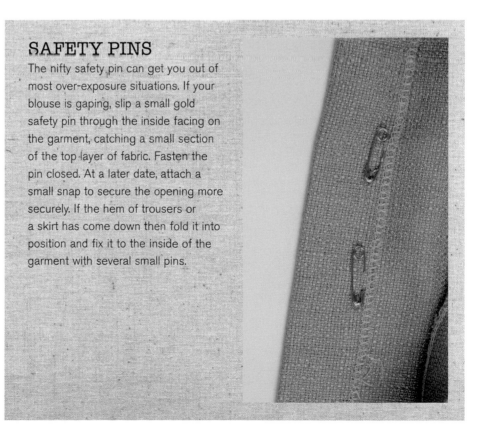

SAFETY PINS

The nifty safety pin can get you out of
most over-exposure situations. If your
blouse is gaping, slip a small gold
safety pin through the inside facing on
the garment, catching a small section
of the top layer of fabric. Fasten the
pin closed. At a later date, attach a
small snap to secure the opening more
securely. If the hem of trousers or
a skirt has come down then fold it into
position and fix it to the inside of the
garment with several small pins.

FABRIC GLUE

Fabric glue is available at most craft and haberdashery shops. There are several different types on the market and they can be very handy for instant repairs to a wide variety of garments and fabrics. Always read the instructions on the packet or bottle to check whether it can be used on the material you need to repair, particularly leather.

Gluing on a leather patch

Getting leather repaired can be very expensive, but to do it yourself can be difficult. If a leather garment is torn then it's advisable to have it professionally repaired, but if the garment is very old or this is not financially viable then a patch glued over the tear may solve the problem. Ready-made leather patches in a variety of colours can be found in good haberdashery stores. As an alternative, adding an embroidered motif can bring a designer look to some leather jackets, if the repair is in a suitable place, at the top of a sleeve or on a breast pocket, for example.

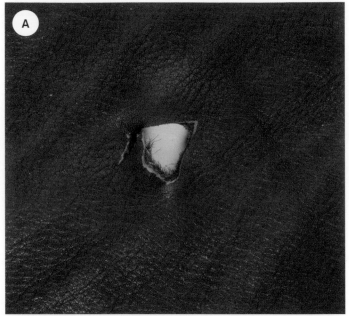

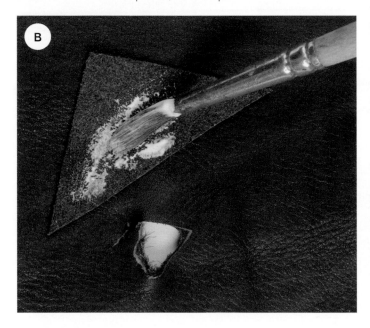

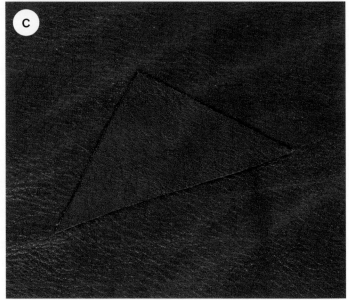

STEP 1

Lay the leather garment face up (**A**). Apply a small amount of glue over the back of the patch (**B**), which needs to be sufficiently larger than the hole or tear in order to adhere to the leather around it.

STEP 2

Wait until the glue becomes tacky and then press the patch over the top of the tear (**C**).

Gluing up a leather hem

If the hem of a leather skirt or jacket needs repairing then fabric glue will do the job quickly and efficiently (no image reference). Using a small paint brush, apply a thin layer of glue onto the inside of the hem, wait until the glue becomes tacky and then press the two layers of leather together. Leave the glue to dry for a few hours before wearing the garment.

BULLDOG CLIPS

If the buttons pop off a knitted cardigan, reach into the office drawer for a bulldog clip. It may look a little unusual, but it could be a good topic of conversation with that cute guy or girl who keeps popping by your desk for a chat!

BROOCHES

Brooches are the perfect solution for an instant fix. They can be used as a decorative replacement for buttons, hooks and clasps. Keep a couple of spare brooches of different sizes in your instant DIY repair kit.

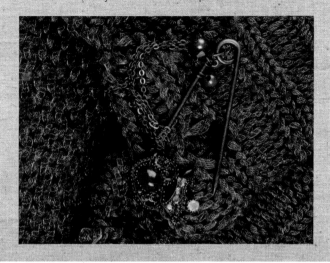

IRON-ON PATCHES

Iron-on patches can be bought from the fabric sections of all good department stores and haberdashery shops, and are available in plain colours or as embroidered motifs. The back of the patch is impregnated with heat-sensitive glue, which, when activated by the iron, adheres to fabric. It is important to read the application instructions before pressing the patch onto the garment.

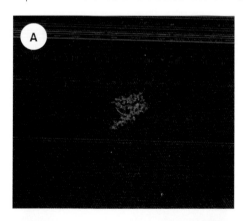

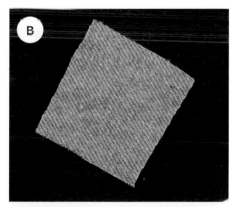

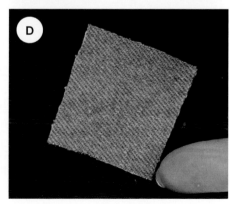

STEP 1

Use a patch in the same type of fabric as the garment you wish to repair, and in a matching colour (a contrasting patch is shown in the step-by-step photographs, for clarity). Set the iron to the recommended heat setting for the fabric. Turn the garment inside out (**A**).

STEP 2

Place the glue side of the iron-on patch over the tear (**B**). Cover the patch with a handkerchief. Press the iron over the covered patch and hold in place for several seconds (**C**).

STEP 3

Check to see if the adhesive has melted sufficiently by trying to lift one corner of the patch (**D**). If it's not completely attached, iron the patch again. Allow the patch to cool before wearing the garment.

IRON-ON DECORATIVE MOTIFS

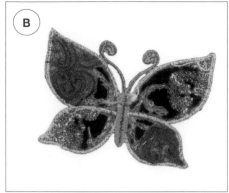

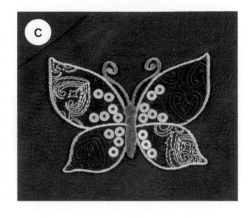

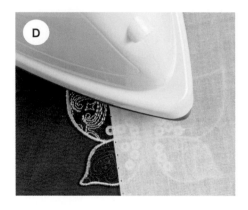

Iron-on decorative motifs come in a huge range of shapes and designs, and often have additional embellishments (**A**). Like plain, iron-on patches, they have heat-activated adhesive on the back (**B**). These motifs can be used to cover tears, holes and permanent stains and are applied like iron-on patches (see page 93), except that they are pressed onto the right side of the material; not the inside, where they would be concealed (**C**).

If the motif you use is embellished with sequins or beads, you will need to place a handkerchief over the top of the motif before ironing to prevent them being damaged (**D**). Crystal-embedded motifs can also be used.

MAKING YOUR OWN DECORATIVE MOTIF

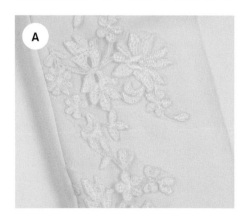

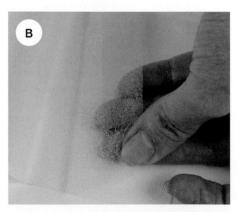

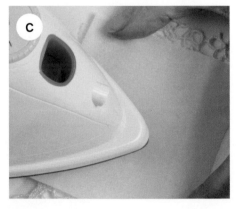

Creating your own decorative motif is very easy – all you need is a suitable piece of fabric or lace (**A**) and some heat-sensitive bonding web, which is available in craft and haberdashery shops. It seals the edges of fabric so that it won't fray once bonded to a garment. Ask for webbing that has a paper backing, as it is easier to use (**B**).

STEP 1
Cut a piece of webbing large enough to cover the fabric you wish to use as a motif. Place the webbing-side down onto the wrong side of the material. Press the paper backing with a warm dry iron. Constantly move the iron over the paper to prevent scorching the fabric (**C**).

STEP 2
Once fused, peel away the paper, trim the webbing to match the shape of the fabric or lace and iron it onto your garment just as you would with a ready-made decorative motif (see above).

PRESS-STICK VELCRO

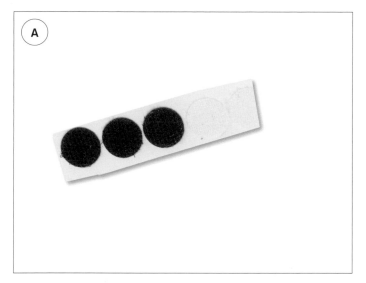

Velcro press-stick dots (**A**) and strips (**B**) are great for emergency repairs. Most supermarkets have a small stand stocked with haberdashery items. Pop a small packet into your desk drawer or the glove compartment of your car. These handy items can be used as an instant fix for a broken zip.

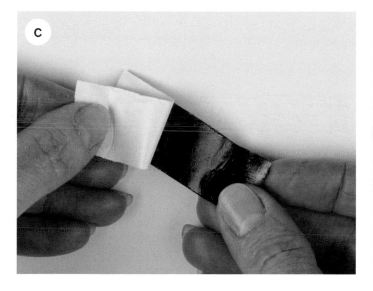

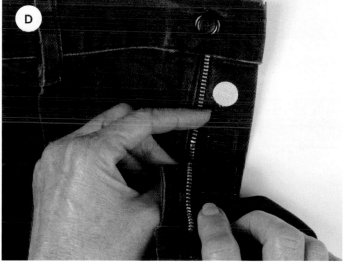

STEP 1
Select the tape and dots you need, cutting the tape to the required length, peel off the backing paper of the rough 'hook' side of the Velcro and stick down firmly onto one side of the closure (**C**).

STEP 2
Apply the soft 'loop' side of the Velcro onto the other side of the closure, ensuring that they are aligned to overlap neatly (**D**).

The use of press-stick Velcro is very much a temporary measure as the adhesive is not nearly as strong as sew-in Velcro (see pages 42–3) or iron-on Velcro (see pages 44–5). Rather than test the permanency of this repair, it is best to change clothes at the earliest opportunity.

Instant Mending

If you snag your shirt or the hem of your skirt and the fabric tears, don't despair. With a little piece of iron-on interfacing the damage can be fixed in a jiffy. Keep a small amount of white and black interfacing on hand for quick repairs.

You Will Need

- Iron-on interfacing
- Scissors
- Iron
- Water-spray bottle
- Handkerchief or pressing cloth

STEP 1

Gently press the torn fabric (**A**) so that the edges of the tear are touching (**B**). Turn the garment inside out.

STEP 2

Cut a piece of iron-on interfacing, slightly wider and longer than the tear in the fabric. Place the interfacing with the pre-glued side over the tear on the inside of the garment (**C**).

STEP 3

Cover the interfacing with a handkerchief or pressing cloth. Spray the covering cloth with a fine mist of water. Now press the iron firmly over the cloth, holding it in place for 30 seconds. Remove the cloth and check that the interfacing is fully adhered to the fabric. If it is not yet fully adhered, repeat the process but do not hold the iron down for more than 30 seconds at a time, in case it should scorch the fabric.

STEP 4

Turn the garment right side out. If there are any frayed strands or fabric fibres showing, trim them off with scissors (**D**).

Darning a Hole

Darning figures pretty high on the drudgery list, right up there with the ironing, but it is such a useful skill to acquire so that you can repair all sorts of little holes or tears in your favourite garments. Put on some music, pour a glass of wine and settle into a comfortable chair to treat yourself while you do that darn darning!

Some little holes or tears can easily be repaired with iron-on interfacing (see pages 96–7). Others can be darned very quickly with a sewing machine. Some garments – those of a more intricate shape, the classic example being a sock with a hole in the toe – still need to be darned by hand.

You Will Need
- Sewing machine
- Thread
- Seam ripper
- Scissors

DARNING WITH A SEWING MACHINE

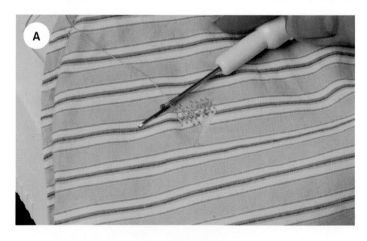

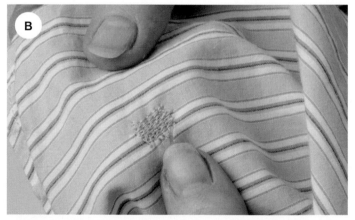

STEP 1
Thread up your sewing machine with sewing thread to match the colour of the fabric (contrasting thread is used in the photographs for clarity) and set it to straight stitch with a small stitch length. Working widthways across the tear on the right side of the fabric, stitch back and forth across the tear, catching a few strands of fabric on each side. Continue until you have covered the tear, working in that one direction. When finished, cut off the end of the thread (**A**).

STEP 2
Turn the fabric approximately 90 degrees, and work back and forth over the original stitches to reinforce the repair. When finished stitching, secure the thread and snip off with scissors (**B**).

DARNING BY HAND

STEP 1
Support the hole in the sock with your hand (**A**) or with a wooden darning dome. Contrasting thread is used in the photographs for clarity.

STEP 2
With a threaded needle, make a series of small running stitches in one direction back and forth to close the hole (**B**).

STEP 3
In the same way, now stitch in the opposite direction to reinforce the repair (**C**). Knot off and trim the thread close to the stitching.

Tip
Always repair a tear or hole before laundering garments made from linen or loose-weave fabrics, as the torn edges will possibly fray and enlarge during the washing process, thus making it more difficult to repair at a later date.

Mending a Pull in Knitted Fabric

A pulled yarn in a favourite knitted garment is not the end of the world. If the yarn is still intact and the stitch hasn't laddered through the rest of the garment, then it can be carefully pulled to the inside and neatly secured; that cosy cardigan or snug jumper can be repaired and enjoyed once again.

You Will Need
- Needle
- Matching thread
- Scissors

STEP 1
Thread a needle and knot the two strands together (contrasting thread is used in the photographs for clarity). Isolate the area of the garment with the snag that you will be repairing (**A**). The snag will most usually be on the outside of the garment. Stitch through the end of the pulled yarn. Make a small back stitch into the yarn to secure the thread into it (**B**).

STEP 2
Take the needle back into the hole from where the yarn was pulled (**C**) through to the inside of the garment (**D**).

STEP 3
Ease the fabric of the garment gently with your fingers to remove any puckering on the outside. Now stitch the yarn to the inside of the garment closing the hole from whence it came, using neat little back stitches (**E**). Trim off any excess thread with scissors. The repair should now be invisible from the outside of the garment (**F**).

Mending a Hole in Stretch Fabric

Stretch fabric isn't all that easy to repair. Once damaged it can ladder or become misshapen. The easiest way to mend a hole in stretch fabric is to cover it from the inside with a patch made from a similar fabric or to glue a decorative patch over the top of the hole.

You Will Need
- Hemming web
- Small patch of matching stretch fabric
- Scissors
- Iron
- Handkerchief or pressing cloth

Tip
You can also cover small holes with an iron-on decorative patch. See page 94 for how to make your own.

STEP 1
Cut a patch of fabric (**A**) sufficient in size to cover the hole in the damaged garment (**B**).

STEP 2
Cut out a piece of iron-on hemming web the same size as the patch. Iron it on to the back of the patch, using a pressing cloth (**C**).

STEP 3
Place the patch on the inside of the garment with the hemming web against the hole (**D**). Cover the patch with a pressing cloth and press it firmly with a warm iron for approximately 20–30 seconds.

STEP 4
Turn the garment right-side out and check that the hole is completely repaired (**E**).

Invisible Mending

If a valuable garment is damaged there are companies that specialize in invisible mending and it is worth doing some internet research into a company that may be able to assist you. For clothing, however, such as coats or jackets that may have been eaten by moths while in winter storage, an almost invisible DIY repair may still be achieved if the hole is very small.

You Will Need
- Dressmaking scissors
- Hemming web
- Small patch of iron-on interfacing
- Baking parchment or Teflon sheet
- Iron

STEP 1
Isolate the small hole you need to repair (**A**). Snip off a little of the fabric from an inside seam allowance where it's not visible (**B**).

STEP 2
Shred the fabric so that you have a little pile of fibres (**C**). Chop up the fibres with scissors so that they become almost a powder (**D**).

STEP 3
Snip tiny shards of hemming web into the fibres and mix them together (**E**). Carefully push the fibre mix into the hole on the garment, using the closed blades of a pair of dressmaking scissors (**F**). Ensure the fibres are flush with the outside of the garment (**G**).

STEP 4
Now place a small piece of hemming web a little larger than the hole on the inside of the garment, covering the repair. This is to fuse the fibres in place. Cover with a Teflon cooking sheet or baking parchment and press with a warm iron (**H**). Move the iron over the covering for about ten seconds. Remove the covering and check that the fibres have melded into the hole.

STEP 5
To finish, press a larger patch of iron-on interfacing over the repaired hole, also on the inside of the garment, to reinforce the repair (**I**).

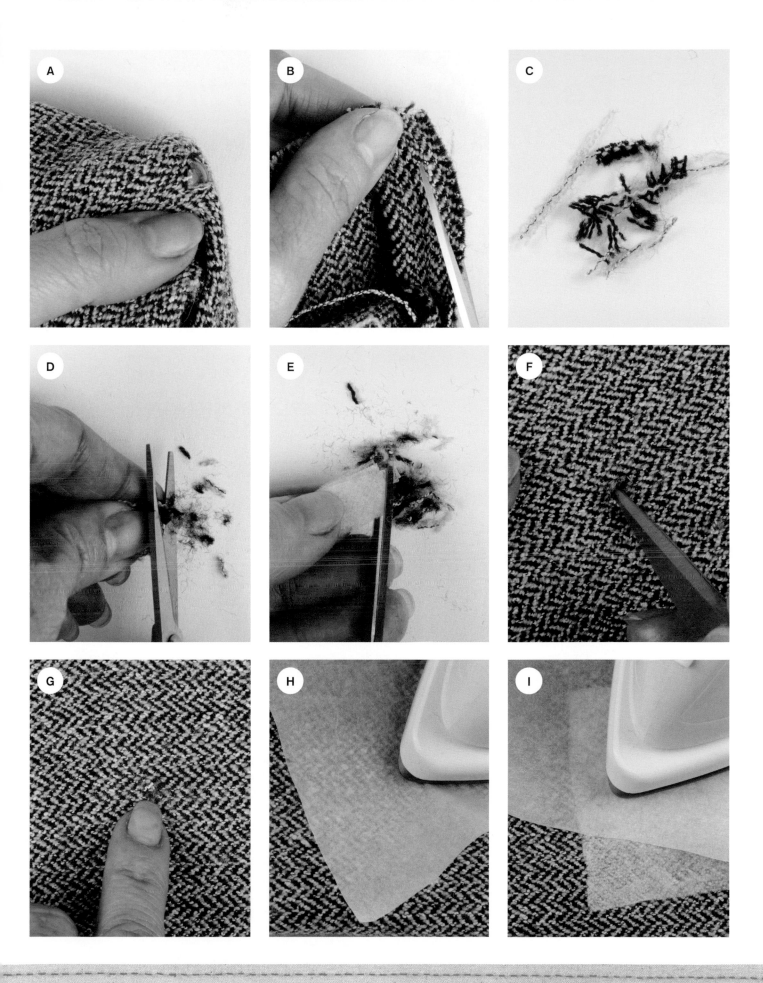

Removing and Mending a Damaged Shirt Pocket

Pockets on a business shirt often become damaged over time, as pens and wallets are slid in and out of them on a daily basis. Pens can also leak into the shirt and pocket fabric or the stitching can gradually become weakened and break through. In such cases, the pockets can either be permanently removed or easily repaired.

You Will Need

- Seam ripper
- Water-spray bottle
- 3fl oz (75ml) distilled water
- ¾fl oz (20ml) white vinegar
- Iron and pressing cloth
- Needle
- Matching thread
- Scissors
- Pins

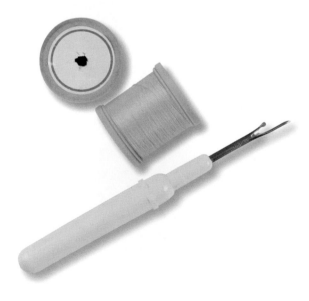

TO COMPLETELY REMOVE A SHIRT POCKET

STEP 1

Using a seam ripper, carefully unpick the stitches from the wrong side of the garment (**A**).

STEP 2

Once all the stitching has been removed, spray the area with a mist of water and press. If there is still a stitch line or 'shadow' of where the pocket was, fill a water-spray bottle with 3fl oz (75ml) of distilled water. Add ¾fl oz (20ml) of white vinegar. Shake well, then spray the fabric with the solution. *NB: Do not spray pure silk or dry-clean only fabrics.* The vinegar helps to remove creases in woven fabrics. Cover the area with a piece of fabric and press.

TO REPAIR A SHIRT POCKET

STEP 1

To repair the stitching on a pocket, pin it back into position (**B**). Thread a needle and tie a knot in one end of the thread (contrasting thread is used in the photographs for clarity). Pass the needle from the inside of the garment to the top surface, stitching over a few of the original stitches with back stitch to secure them.

STEP 2

Continue to sew with neat, small and evenly tensioned back stitches until the pocket is firmly back into place (**C**). Knot off the thread neatly on the inside of the shirt.

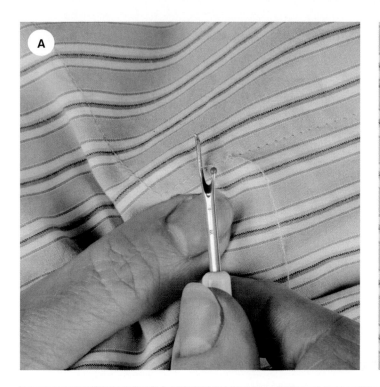

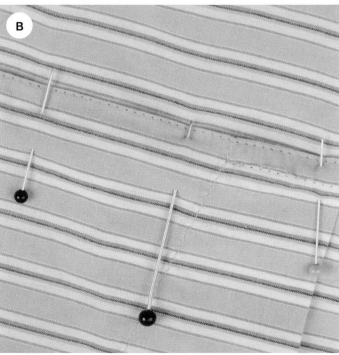

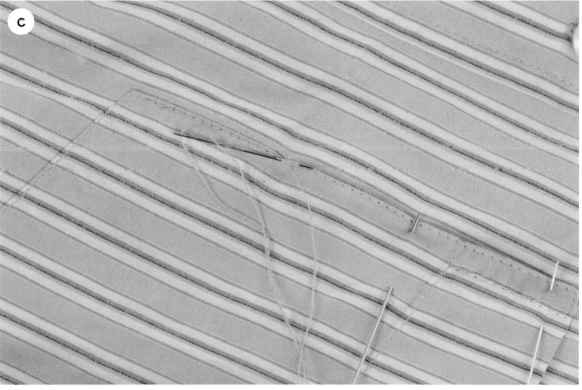

Expanding a Waistband

To expand the waistband on a skirt or pair of trousers can be as simple as moving the button or metal closure so that you have a little more ease in the band to provide a more comfortable fit. Not everyone has a waist measurement that will fit ready-made clothing perfectly, so moving the button can make quite a difference.

You Will Need
- Scissors
- Needle
- Matching thread
- Water-soluble fabric marker pen
- Seam ripper

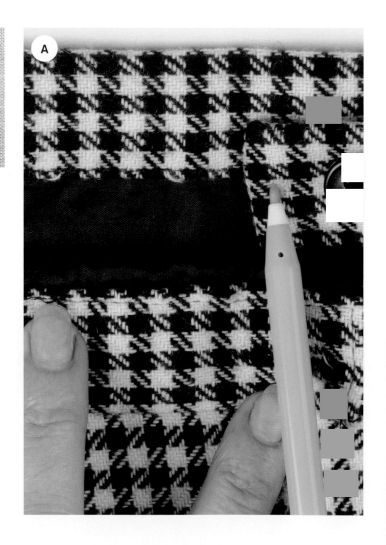

STEP 1
Try on the garment. If the zip closes comfortably to the top of the skirt or trousers then you're in luck: the body of the garment fits you, it's just the waistband that is too tight. Using a fabric marker pen, mark on the waistband the new position for the button or closure, perhaps right out at the end of the waistband (**A**).

STEP 2
Remove the button or metal closure with a seam ripper or sharp scissors (**B**).

STEP 3
Sew on the button or metal closure to the new position marked on the waistband (contrasting thread is used here for clarity) (**C**).

STEP 4
Then secure the thread to the inside of the waistband (**D**). You have now given yourself a little bit more breathing room at the waist (**E**)!

Reducing a Waistband

The easiest way to reduce the waistband on a skirt or pair of trousers is to slash the waistband open and unpick the back seam of the garment. This is assuming that the back seam doesn't include a zip. If the back seam does have a zip then you will need to reduce the waistband at the side seams of the garment.

You Will Need
- Seam ripper
- Scissors
- Needle
- Matching thread
- Pins
- Dressmaking chalk or water-soluble fabric marker pen
- Fray-stop glue
- Button or metal fastener hook and eye (if using)

STEP 1
Try the garment on inside out. Pin the extra fabric of the waistband either in the back seam or divided equally at the two side seams. Mark the new stitching line with fabric marker pen or dressmaking chalk. If you are making this alteration down the single back seam, remove the closures from the waistband using a seam ripper, and set them aside until step 5.

STEP 2
Carefully cut through the waistband to reach the stitching of the seam allowance. Unpick the stitching of the seam allowance from the waistline down into the seam(s) for at least 5in (13cm) (**A**).

STEP 3
Pin in the new seam following the marks on the inside of the garment that you made in step 1 (**B**). Pin the excess fabric from the top of the seam to match the amount you wish to reduce from the waistband. Gradually pin down the seam, easing back out onto to the original seam.

STEP 4
Now pin the waistband back onto the garment, using the marks as your guide (**C**). Try the garment on before stitching the waistband and back or side seams securely together, using either back stitch or a sewing machine. Run a little fray-stop glue over the raw edges of the cut waistband to stop the fabric from fraying.

STEP 5
If you have made this alteration down the single back seam of the garment, you will now need to reattach the waistband closures (button or metal fastener hook and eye) to the ends of the new, shortened waistband.

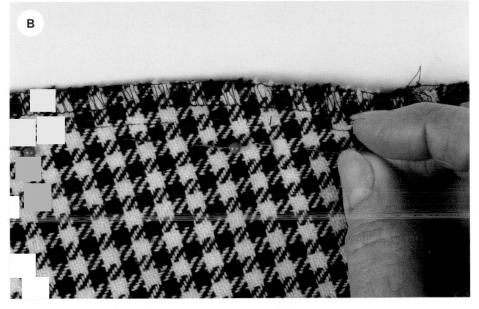

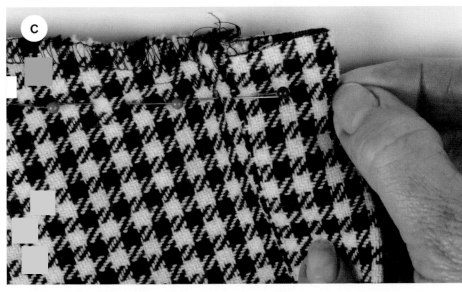

Replacing a Drawstring

If the drawstring in the waistband of a garment, such as tracksuit bottoms, has not been overstitched and it pulls out of the casing then it is quite a simple procedure to reinsert it into the waistband – and to prevent it working its way out again.

STEP 1
Attach a safety pin to one end of the drawstring (**A**).

STEP 2
Insert the safety-pinned end of the drawstring into one of the holes and, using the safety pin to hold on to, gather the waistband fabric over the string (**B**), working it all the way round the waistband and out the other opening (**C**).

STEP 3
Create a large knot in each end of the drawstring (**D**) or thread on a bead and knot it in place to prevent the string from sliding inside the casing and working its way out again.

You Will Need
- Scissors
- Safety pin
- 2 beads (optional)

Tip
Elastic may be threaded into the casing in a similar way and secured with a few quick stitches.

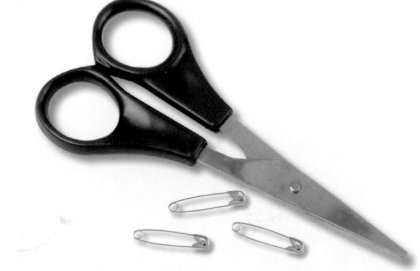

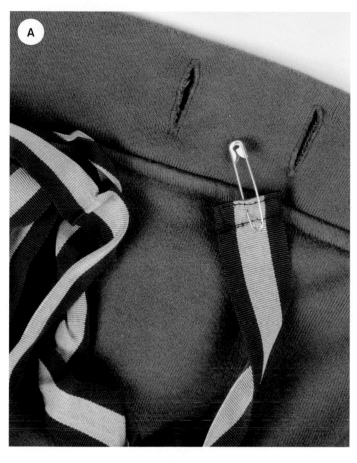

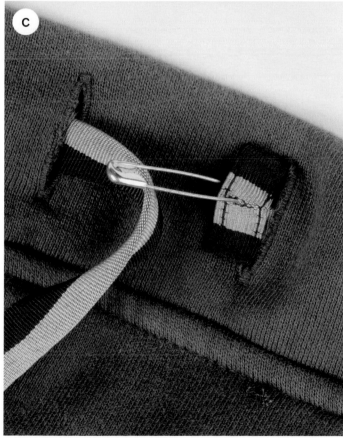

Fixing a Zip Pull

Zip pulls often dislodge from the top of the zip through wear and tear. You can replace a zip pull with another metal one or create your own fashion statement by attaching a bead or toggle to a jumpring.

You Will Need
- Zip pull
- Chain-nose pliers
- Flat-nose pliers
- Needle
- Thread
- Beads or toggle
- Fray-stop glue

STEP 1
Open the jaws of the zip pull with chain-nose pliers, just sufficiently to clip it onto the zip (**A**).

STEP 2
Thread the ring back onto the zip pull. Holding one end of the ring in each pair of pliers, realign the ends to form a continuous ring (**B**). Squeeze the jaws of the zip pull closed with either pair of pliers.

STEP 3
Thread a needle with a double length of strong thread. Thread some decorative beads onto the needle (**C**) to create a row of the desired length. Pass the length of beads through the ring on the zip pull (**D**).

STEP 4
Thread the needle back through the row of beads (or the toggle if using) and then knot off and secure with fray stop (**E**).

Tip
Ready-made zip pulls can be purchased from bead shops and most haberdashery shops.

B

C

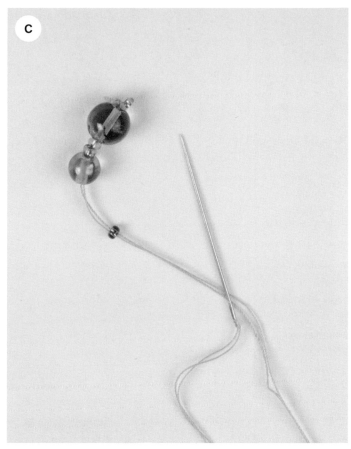

D

E

Suppliers

UK

Michael Abakhan Ltd
Coast Road
Llanerch-y-Mor
Mostyn
Nr Holywell
CH8 9DX
Tel: +44 (0)1745 562 100
www.abakhan.co.uk

Fred Aldous Ltd
37 Lever Street
Manchester
M1 1LW
Tel: +44 (0)1621 236 4224
www.fredaldous.co.uk

C & H Fabrics
179 Western Road
Brighton
BN1 2BA
Tel: +44 (0)1273 321 959
www.candh.co.uk

Janome Sewing Machines
Janome Centre
Southside
Stockport
Cheshire
SK6 2SP
Tel: +44 (0)161 666 6011
www.janome.co.uk

Jaycotts
Unit D2
Chester Trade Park
Bumpers Lane
Chester
CH1 4LT
Tel: +44 (0)1244 394 099
www.jaycotts.co.uk

John Kaldor Fabricmaker (UK) Ltd
Centro 4
20–23 Mandela Street
Camden
London
NW1 0DU
Tel: +44 (0)20 7874 5070
www.johnkaldor.co.uk

John Lewis
Oxford Street
London
W14 1EX
Tel: +44 (0)20 7629 7711
www.johnlewis.com

Remnant Kings
146 Argyle Street
Glasgow
G2 8BL
Tel: +44 (0)141 221 2220
www.remnantkings.co.uk

The Stitchery
12–16 Riverside Cliffe Bridge
High Street
Lewes
BN7 2RE
Tel: +44 (0)1273 473 557
www.the-stitchery.co.uk

Some more online suppliers are:
www.calicolaine.co.uk
www.habbyworld.co.uk
www.hobbycraft.co.uk
www.jaytrim.com
www.ladysewandsew.co.uk
www.millcroftextiles.co.uk
www.ribbonmoon.co.uk
www.sewing.co.uk
www.sewingcrafts.co.uk
www.sewingmachines.co.uk
www.simplicity.com
www.truetrim.com

USA

Brewer Quilting & Sewing Supplies
3702 Prairie Lake Court
Aurora
IL 60504
Tel: +1 630 820 5695
www.brewersewing.com

Britex Fabrics
146 Geary Street
San Francisco
CA 94108
Tel: +1 415 392 2910
www.britexfabrics.com

Gutermann of America Inc
24 American Street
PO Box 507
Mount Holly
NC 28120
Tel: +1 704 525 7068
www.gutermann.com

Janome Sewing Machines
10 Industrial Avenue
Mahwah
NJ 07430
Tel: +1 800 631 0183
www.janome.com

Joann fabric and craft stores
(Stores nationwide)
www.joann.com
Tel (toll free): +1 888 739 4120

Michaels
(Stores nationwide)
www.michaels.com

Sil Thread Inc
257 W 38th Street
NY 10018
Tel: +1 212 997 8949
www.threadus.com

AUSTRALIA

Lincraft
60 Fulton Drive
Derriment
3030 VIC
Tel: +61 1300 546 272
www.lincraft.com.au

Spotlight
Head Office
111 Cecil Street
South Melbourne
3205 VIC
Tel: +61 1300 305 405
www.spotlight.com.au

SOUTH AFRICA

Habby & Lace
56 Voortrekker Street
Vereeniging
Tel: +27 16 422 5400
www.habbyandlace.co.za

Lifestyle Fabrics, Curtain and Linen
11 Picton Street
Parow
Cape Town
Tel: +27 21 930 5170
www.lifestylefabrics.co.za

NEW ZEALAND

Moreland Fabrics
23 Veronica Street
New Lynn
AKL 0600
Tel: +64 9 826 3075
https://morelandfabrics.co.nz

Spotlight
The Colombo
363 Colombo Street
Sydenham
CAN 8023
Tel: +64 3 377 6121
www.spotlightstores.com.nz

Index

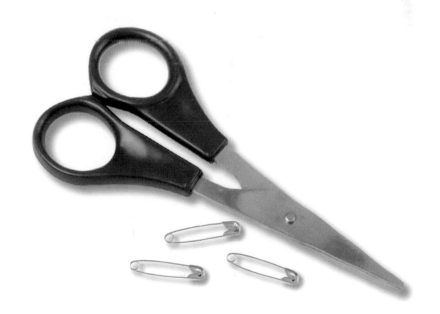

Index

To place an order, or to request a catalogue, contact:
GMC Publications Ltd
Castle Place, 166 High Street, Lewes, East Sussex, BN7 1XU
United Kingdom
Tel: +44 (0)1273 488005
www.gmcbooks.com